GENEVIEVE ANTOINE DARIAUX

The Men
in
Your Life

TIMELESS ADVICE AND
WISDOM ON MANAGING
THE OPPOSITE SEX

WILLIAM MORROW
An Imprint of HarperCollins Publishers

This edition was published in 2004 by HarperCollins Publishers UK.
It was first published in Great Britain in 1968 by Frederick Muller Ltd.

HarperCollins books may be purchased for educational, business, or
sales promotional use. For information please write: Special Markets
Department, HarperCollins Publishers, 10 East 53rd Street,
New York, NY 10022.

FIRST U.S. EDITION

Printed on acid-free paper

Library of Congress Cataloging-in-Publication Data

Antoine Dariaux, Genevieve.
    The men in your life: timeless advice and wisdom on managing
the opposite sex / by Genevieve Antoine Dariaux.
        p. cm.
    Originally published: London: Muller, 1968.
    ISBN 13: 978-0-06-084625-1 (alk. paper)
    ISBN 10: 0-06-084625-9
    1. Women. 2. Men. 3. Man-woman relationships. I. Title.

HQ1221.A58   2006
306.7—dc22   2005050481

06 07 08 09 10 RRD 10 9 8 7 6 5 4 3 2 1

The Men in Your Life

To my husband, to my boss, and to all the other men who have been or who I wish had been in my life.

Contents

Preface

The Men in Your Life – what a fascinating subject! Whenever I have mentioned the title of this book, not a single man or woman has failed to respond with an 'Oh, oh!' filled with innuendo and a wicked gleam in the eye. Each time I must remind people that men are not only lovers but also fathers, sons and policemen.

Dare I confess that there have been very few men in my life? I am a professional in the fashion field and a very experienced hostess, but where men are concerned I have had just one grandfather until the age of fifteen, a father who was divorced and lived far away, no brothers or brothers-in-law, not even a father-in-law, and neither of the men I would so love to have known: a son and a son-in-law. I have had sufficient beaux to feel no regret, but not so many as to feel remorse, only two employers and one husband – it really isn't very much! But perhaps it is because I have had so few men in my family that men interest me so much.

I must even confess that when I started to write this book I believed that men were far superior to women, and that the matriarchy toward which we were heading would be a disastrous abyss. I was a bit dazzled by Michelangelo, Johann Sebastian Bach and Voltaire, and I could think of no women of comparable genius. Then, after further reflection, I was obliged to admit that men have always done everything in their power to prevent women from developing their potentialities in order to retain them in their service, and that Lamartine would probably never have written *The Lake* if the only expanse of water he had ever contemplated was in the kitchen sink.

Nevertheless, it seems to me that, having acquired a certain rather favourable equilibrium with men – and complete equality thanks to The Pill – we ought to allow some form of masculine authority for our own sake, because if we take this last support away from them we will have only puppets as husbands and companions. Real women can only love real men, for woman needs man in order to bloom just as a plant requires a support to withstand wind and storms. So let's take good care of our men and play them right – they are still the most interesting things in our lives!

The Men in Your Life

ABSENCE

Like a double-edged blade, the absence of a loved one can make you discover either that you can get along without him very well, or that without him even the Mediterranean sky seems grey. It is therefore indispensable to get away from the man in your life for a while in order to make sure that that is what he really is. But you must be honest with yourself. The absence of the man you love is a heart-rending thing, and not merely the problem of keeping your feet warm when you sleep alone; it is a constant sensation of bleakness, and not the discomfort of having to change your daily habits.

After many years of marriage, it is not a bad idea for couples to separate occasionally, if only in order to miss the mannerisms which annoy you every day and for which you will have greater indulgence when you accept them as part of your life. It is, in fact, the only way of learning that you cannot fall asleep without the lullaby of your husband's snores!

However, if you are not very sure of your hold on

your husband, you must think twice before giving him a chance to see how much more fun life can be without you. Above all, if you simply have to leave him for a certain length of time, don't let him go home to his mother; delighted to recover her little boy, she will soon manage to reaccustom him to all the comforts of his childhood: his favourite foods, his clothes pressed every day, etc. – comforts which you have had enough trouble trying to make him forget. If your absence should lead him to make comparisons, you must therefore arrange things so that they are all in your favour . . . which means that he will have to suffer a little.

But if you feel in a joyous holiday mood the moment he leaves you alone – if you are not too old, have no children and possess an independent income, I think that it is time to look for another mate, for he is no longer anything but a habit in your life instead of the half he ought to be.

ACCESSORIES

There is no point in saying that 'clothes do not make the man'. They still represent one aspect of a man, and it is the one that determines what kind of first impression he makes.

And so, mesdames, since it is rare for men to buy all these trinkets for themselves and since they generally count on your generosity, lump together Christmas, their birthdays, and your wedding anniversary and give them only the very best of each type of article. Men are just as impressed as we are by a prestigious label, so remember that in the long run a necktie from Harvey Nichols costs very little more than one selected from the small shop round the corner.

ACTORS

Every women in the civilized world has her favourite actor. She is madly in love with him when she is very young, and a little more vaguely later on, when she has real-life love affairs to get her teeth into. But she often remains faithful throughout her entire life to the same type of man as the one who so impressed her as a child. This phenomenon is, moreover, identical with men, who always choose from the same category of women, simply taking a more recent model; in fact, it is always rather surprising that a man who divorces a dizzy blonde with whom he was miserably unhappy doesn't throw himself at the first Andalusian who passes by with blazing eyes, swarthy as a prune and steeped in sanctity – but no, he inevitably chooses an exact replica of his first wife!

An actor therefore occupies a very important place in women's lives. He populates their dreams, even the ones they dream by day, and many a husband owes more passionate embraces to Cary Grant than to his own over-familiar charms. At the same time, the husbands are perhaps thinking of Brigitte Bardot in order to work up their courage.

An actor has already inspired so many sensations in you that if you met him in real life you would have the impression of meeting an old friend, especially if he has often been in your home when you were in your nightgown – in other words, on television. A friend even told me that his mother, who is almost a hundred years old and a rabid television fan, complains of no longer being able to undress in her bedroom because it is always full of men!

It is therefore difficult to imagine that an actor is a man like any other, who makes an entrance on the stage just as your husband goes to his office, when to you he is the incarnation of Don Juan. You are, moreover, not entirely mistaken. A famous actor is *not* a man like any other. He is much more sensitive, but also much more vulnerable, and he is usually impossible to live with because he is completely egocentric. He needs compliments even more than an ordinary man, and that is saying a lot! Not only does criticism flay him, but silence scalps him. Like a foetus bathed in the amniotic fluid of its mother's womb, he can survive only in a pool of public adoration. From time to time he plays a comedy of passion for his own pleasure and tries to turn it into his best role, but he often tires of it long before the thousandth performance, and one even wonders why certain actors go to the bother of getting officially married each time. They are so used to imitating every emotion that from time to time they put on grand scenes of hatred or of vengeance as well. He knows that popularity, like fashion, is ephemeral and that he must ensure his future. As a matter of fact, many young actors take advantage of their moment of glory to marry heiresses who will serve as a sort of social security and retirement fund for their old age. And so, mesdemoiselles, I cannot warn you too strongly: you are running a great risk in marrying a member of the acting profession, if you are not one yourself. Personally, I prefer a husband who does not inspire too many dreams in other women.

Unless you move in artistic circles and are in the habit of meeting actors very often, you have very little chance of capturing their interest, for in general they are happy only among themselves or in the company of people who are very well informed about the field or of journalists who can be of help to them.

So do not be too sad if, given the choice between a beautiful, passionately enamoured fan who has moved mountains in order to meet her favourite star and a little tenth-rate cross-eyed lady journalist, he prefers to go to supper with the latter in order to get a line in the *Gazette*! Still, the only attitude that is sure to please an actor is one of wide-eyed admiration.

Young girls who scramble for autographs or write passionate letters to an actor now make me smile with indulgence and a little pity, because it is certain that some secretary will be quite unmoved by their tear-stained missives. While some actors loudly complain of being slaves to the public you can be sure that they become very alarmed the moment their fan mail starts to drop off. So, dear young friends, if you want to maintain the morale of your favourite film star, continue to proclaim your love as loudly as possible; it will help him to land contracts. Besides, there are, alas, not many occasions in life for dreaming – you will get over it.

ADMIRATION

Admiration is as indispensable to life as oxygen. Even a puppy wriggles with joy when you tell him how handsome he is.

It is not only because of the sunshine that it is more pleasant to stroll along a street in Italy than in England. It is also because in Italy all the men look at you and say that you are beautiful, whereas in England it is considered poor taste to raise an eyebrow at a passing woman – even at Lady Godiva naked on her horse. Come to think of it, I don't know any other country where that famous beauty would have remained on her mount for more than five minutes!

All human beings are actors who long to be applauded: the ambitious by the entire world, the modest by only a few, the wise by themselves alone.

Even if you are the most egocentric person in the world as well as the most beautiful (and the two often go together), the only way of finding happiness is to redistribute among all the men who surround you some of the homage they so generously strew at your feet.

In any case, you should never:

1. marry someone you do not admire
2. marry someone who does not admire you
3. work for an employer you do not consider admirable
4. work for an employer who does not appreciate you

ADULTERY

First of all, let's be honest: the word is much uglier than the deed. It is a technical term which, like all the rest of them, lacks poetry. Speak to me of 'escapade', of 'weakness', of 'passing fancy', of 'love at first sight'; but 'adultery' – horrors!

From a religious point of view it is one of the seven capital sins, in the same category as murder. And even today, in certain civilizations, people will readily throw stones at an adulterous woman, while they rally to the defence of a man who has killed a rival allegedly in order to save his honour. Naturally, in these same civilizations, the idea of an adulterous man doesn't even exist.

Thank heavens, in our age and in our world there has been a great deal of progress and we no longer so much as point an accusing finger at a person guilty of adultery. Centuries of theatrical comedies entirely based on the theme of a triangular or quadrangular ménage have even taught us to find it funny. And yet when it happens to you, you seldom feel like laughing.

Let's examine a few typical cases and see what might be the best attitude to take towards them.

1. The most common case: the momentary, purely physical attraction of a man who is removed from his family environment, who has eaten a good dinner and finishes off the evening by cutting a few capers with a lady of easy virtue.

Nine times out of ten you will never learn about it, because it occurs during a business trip; and nine times out of ten you will even obtain as a result a little gift that your remorseful spouse will buy the next morning. But if some chance indiscretion or blunder brings the incident to your attention, instead of making a drama out of it you should simply laugh off the prowess of your husband. You have here the most propitious moment for getting anything you want out of him – perhaps even breakfast in bed for a year.

2. The case, still quite common but much more disturbing, of the man who has an 'affair' with a woman whom he meets every day.

(a) If it is the children's piano teacher or your best friend, change her for another one immediately.

(b) If it is his secretary or an employee at the office everything becomes much trickier. Here, there are two possible eventualities:

(i) He carefully conceals his liaison, which means that he is ashamed of it and that he is more attached to you than to his filing-clerk siren.

Of course, you suspect nothing. You are always perfectly groomed, made up, and happy; you organize dates and parties and intimate candle-lit dinners for two; you buy a devastating négligé and boldly make advances to him – in short, you do not leave him alone for a single second. You can always take a nap in the afternoon while he is at the office, but he will soon become so exhausted that his girl-friend will seem like overtime labour rather than a distraction.

(ii) He openly flaunts his liaison, which is always frowned upon in every office and therefore means that his new passion is more important to him than his career. This is *serious*.

There is no longer any question of hiding your head under your wing; a heart-to-heart discussion is necessary. But it should be a discussion between partners in the same business, like a brief that you have carefully prepared, clearly presented, without shedding a single tear; this will surely be more effective than tragic imprecations. Futile questions, such as 'What does she have that I haven't got?' (probably twenty years less) will not bring you closer to a solution, because even if he told you it wouldn't make you any happier. If you show him calmly that he is certainly going to lose his job, or two million votes in the next election, that in any case you intend to keep the house, the children, the dog, and most of his salary which your lawyer is sure to obtain for you, but that if he immediately drops the girl you will never mention the episode again – there is still a very good chance that he will think it over.

If he obstinately persists in his folly, you can also refuse a divorce until he has seen the light or, on the contrary, start at once to look for a partner who will appreciate you at your true value. It is a question of temperament, up-bringing or religion, which I shall scrupu-lously refrain from discussing since my only object here, mesdames, is to give you a few recipes for making the best use of these gentlemen.

You have certainly wondered why it is much less accept-able for a woman to treat herself to a blond Adonis when she feels like it than for her husband to offer himself the services of a call girl.

Women's psychology has always enrobed, enribboned and enflowered the sexual act with all sorts of sentiments, emotions and rites that generally excite them much more than the act itself.

The obvious conclusion is, madame, that it is far more serious a matter for you to be unfaithful to your husband than it is for him to be unfaithful to you, since it is very rare for you to attach as little importance to it as he does. So before you fall into the muscular embrace of your ski instructor, it is essential that you be modern enough to be able to do so without the slightest romantic notion in the back of your head. And honest by now, can you?

(See also Affairs, Fidelity, Mistress)

ADVICE

Always ask a man for his advice but never give him yours – unless he asks for it and unless it concerns such minor questions as interior decoration, etiquette, or what to wear.

But if your husband – that natural protector who ought to know everything and to solve all your problems – condescends to follow your advice concerning the colour of his new car (if he consults you as the *make* of car, it is very disturbing and you must take him to the psychiatrist), it is undoubtedly because he doesn't quite have the courage to order it in red, and he wants to shove the responsibility on to you.

It is most difficult of all to refrain from giving advice to your son, especially when he introduces the girl of his dreams to you. A woman must be really awfully civilized in order to like her daughter-in-law; it is not a natural sentiment. But if you believe in all objectivity that your son has made a disastrous choice, instead of telling him so – which would only serve to estrange him from you and to precipitate the wedding – call all his friends to the rescue and set traps for the little bird. You have a host of advantages over her: experience, money, power and maternal love.

At the office, the best ways of making yourself unpopular in the least time are: to give advice to your boss; to take credit for every success and to point out that you predicted every failure; and, needless to add, the truer it is, the less you are likely to be forgiven.

Don't forget that giving advice means undertaking to influence the course of destiny of another person and to commit yourself to seeing that it succeeds. Women who give advice irresponsibly are just as reprehensible as people who sign bad cheques.

AFFAIRS

I am not referring here to business affairs but to the affairs that a woman can have and not handle. It is amusing to think that the English borrowed the word from the French exclusively in the former sense.

What exactly does it mean to have an affair with a man? It is a liaison lasting longer than a night and less than a lifetime; it is basically a bedtime story rather than a love story.

A man has a tendency to manage a love affair like a business affair, which is the only true kind in his eyes. He hops into bed as promptly as he presides over a sales meeting, and he never forgets an appointment.

For a woman, an affair has greater importance. She thinks about it, she dresses very carefully even if only to undress again; she would also like to have time to talk, to be coaxed; sentimentally speaking, she finds it all a bit rapid and a little crude. She sighs . . . but she is there at six o'clock.

(See also Adultery, Fidelity, Mistress)

AFFECTATION

I am extremely suspicious of an affected man: he is surely either a mediocre person who would like to convince people of his success, a *nouveau riche* who would like to have people forget his modest origin, or a sourpuss who bears a grudge against the entire world because he is not rich or famous.

You can sometimes forgive a very pretty woman for being affected in her manners, but an affected man is as irritating as a mosquito buzzing around your head . . . and fills me with the same murderous impulses.

AGE

While few men sell their souls to the devil in exchange for eternal youth like Dr Faustus, more and more of them dip into their capital in order to have their faces lifted. And how can you expect them to resist the indecent advertising glorifying youthfulness? Years ago, honours and responsibilities were inaccessible before the age of fifty, and a Cabinet Minister – or, even more unlikely, a President of the United States – who was barely forty years old was unheard of. When a man was no longer able to run after a tennis ball, he had the compensation of a director's chair in which to repose his expansive girth, which was one of the marks of a success man. With the husband's Legion of Honour came a weekend house in the country. The children were married off in grand style and their parents settled down comfortably in the role of indulgent grandparents. But today people would rather die than appear old. Our fifty-year-olds work like fury to earn still more money, and instead of taking an afternoon nap he does exercises in preparation for the coming ski season – all of which, moreover, kills him.

Even without the slightest effort a man always looks younger than a woman of the same age, and his physiological privilege of being able to procreate for at least twenty years longer encourages him to exchange his original mate for a fresher one. What does it matter if the latter only marries him for his money, figuring that she will still have time to be a very pretty widow? What does it matter if, in order to keep up with her in bed, he must expend his last drop of strength? He conquered time and proved to himself that he was still a young man.

If this frenzy takes hold of your ageing companion, I don't really know what advice to give you, because it's not by dyeing your hair and learning the latest dance steps that you will hang on to him, for he craves only tender young flesh. Perhaps you can try asking his doctor to warn him. Or you can invite your children's friends home more often, so that he finds what he is seeking and at the same time sees its drawbacks. I really don't know. I think, unfortunately, that there is not very much you can do except feel sorry for him.

An Italian friend of mine has discovered a few truths which she has been kind enough to pass on to me:

'Men need our feminine qualities to add cheer to their old age, when they are weighed down by responsibilities and the struggles of life. They are haunted by a desire to escape, fascinated by an impossible ideal of happiness, continually seeking a Lost Paradise. They deceive themselves by conquering the world through the power of money and the illusion of domination. Tired of fighting windmills, they must find a refuge from their solitude in the simplicity of our behaviour as compassionate women and find in us the qualities of maturity and at the same time the carefree spirit of youthfulness. So . . . women must know how to be happy.

'Don't ignore death – it is the stimulant of our vitality and our ardent desire to live.

'We should observe nature with wonder and attention, as if we were seeing it for the first time.

'We must get used to the idea of growing old and accept it joyfully, after having weighed in the balance the advantages of age.

'We must not be influenced by the solicitude and the

disturbing pity of young people, and we should refuse to take their arms when crossing the street.'

Her conclusion is that 'at the springtime of our lives, our souls are masked by our bodies; when autumn comes, we must generate a renaissance. It is when we are young that we suffer moments of despair; thanks to our maturity when we are older, we are freed from most of our complexes, with the result that we are able to see the bright side of life.'

I am sure that we may all envy this marvellous friend who has received a gift from heaven: the key to the art of growing old.

AIR

Although the word 'air' is evocative of freshness, it can be a burning subject between a married couple.

– One partner cannot sleep unless the window is open, and the other catches cold in the slightest draught.

Solution: Separate bedrooms.

– He claims that it is possible to live on air.

Solution: Don't marry him. And if it is already too late, make him buy the groceries.

– He has a tendency to put on airs.

Solution: Deflate him in private, but never in public.

Finally, be extremely wary of the 'air of resemblance' you think you detect in the features of children of new acquaintances. The current husband may not be their father.

ALIBI

Alibi is a Latin word meaning 'elsewhere'. You must organize your alibis very carefully, and preferably choose a girl-friend who is difficult to pin down. You should also verify the closing hours of museums, and before launching into a description of the film you didn't see, you should at least read a detailed review. Do not impose too much on your friends by asking them to confirm your alibis with bare-faced lies – they may not enjoy it. But it is nevertheless indispensable to warn your friends whenever you use them as an alibi, so that they will not involuntarily betray you afterwards.

The best alibi of all is one that is impossible to verify (I am, of course, excluding housebreakers and assassins). So starting today, you might get into the habit of visiting museums, walking in the park, or spending a few hours in the reading-room of the public library. If you are really in the habit of doing all this, nothing is simpler than to do it once more fictitiously, and in the meantime you will at least learn something or get a little exercise.

ALIMONY

A woman certainly has to have a saintly character in order to feel no irritation when a good part of her husband's salary disappears into the pockets of one or more ex-wives, and before marrying a divorced man you should consider this eventuality. However, once you have accepted the situation, it would be in very bad taste to reproach your new husband, or to groan each time he signs a cheque for the expenses of his previous marriage. (See also Ex-Husbands)

ALWAYS

You can believe in it. In fact, you ought to believe in it quite often, because once in a while it's true!

AMBITION

The marriage vows ought to include, in addition to the promise to share each other's joys and pains, a promise to share each other's ambitions.

To take just one example of ambition: if your husband is convinced that the nation needs his enlightened vision and that if he is not elected at least councillor of his borough life won't be worth living, you should know what is in store for you. Even if public life, in your view, holds not the slightest attraction, you must wear a professional smile from morning till night and devote yourself relentlessly to every living creature of voting age, even if you like only babies and dogs. You must always be reassuring, neat but not too fashionable, more maternal than pin-up in style. On the other hand, the younger, handsomer and more telegenic your husband is, the better are his chances. So try not to be jealous of his success with women and console yourself with the thought that it is thanks to these charming ladies that he will be elected. And when he has finally won the office he coveted, you should also know that he will have to work so hard in order not to lose it that he will no longer have time for you – or rather, no more than the time it takes to pose for magazine and newspaper photographs. With all my heart, I hope that this life appeals to you as much as it does to him, because otherwise, if your ambition was to make jam in summer and to toast chestnuts in winter while serenely watching the years go by, it would have been better to have found a different husband.

But if it is you who are obsessed by the dazzling life of the Jet Set, if the only part of the newspaper that interests you is the society page, if your husband refuses to join the golf club which (you mistakenly believe) would be the first rung on the ladder leading to the paradise of a weekend at St Andrews, and persists in liking football, rugger and cricket, and if the nice little life he offers you is beginning to get you down, there are two solutions open to you: leave him and try to get a job as secretary to one of those fabulous persons whose activities fill the pages of the snob magazines, and I bet that within a year you will realize how empty is the existence of these slaves to pleasure, and you will miss the little shingled house where you could at least do as you pleased; or stay with him and patiently try to change his tastes by choosing more cultured friends, by reading something other than the society columns, and by becoming an authority on taste and etiquette among your own circle of friends. You must always be aware of your limitations, and if you absolutely insist on being a social leader, content yourself with being first-class in Southend-on-Sea rather than second-class in London.

But first of all, never marry a man whose ambitions you do not share or who doesn't understand your own.

ANGEL

'Mary, be an angel and get me my shirt!'

'Mother, be an angel and sew on this button for me!'

If you have been an angel all day long, when evening comes you'll find that you are dead on your feet but you haven't yet grown wings.

ANNIVERSARIES

Why is it that even the busiest women always remember anniversaries, while men always forget them? Do they perhaps feel deep in their hearts that there isn't any reason to deck the house with flags just because it is a certain number of years since they paid us the honour of marrying us, and that they would be better off if they had broken a leg on that particular day? I don't know . . . But I do know that if nobody tactfully reminds them of a special date, forget, and they will try to atone by wearing a look of utter mortification when they find a present on the dinner-plate. And so, rather than run the risk of turning an idyllic evening into a tearful scene, I think that it is preferable to play safe and remind your husband a week beforehand that 'next Wednesday is our wedding anniversary'. You can also write all the important dates of the year in his new diary on the first of January. It is a waste of time to weep over typically masculine failings. It is better to try to teach a husband a few good rules of conduct, such as: I give you a silk scarf, and you give me a cashmere one . . . on the right date.

APOLOGIES

Never wait for a reproach before making an apology. Unless you are dealing with a sadist, if you arrive with head hung low to say to your father, your husband or your boss: 'I've done something stupid', they will be much less disagreeable about it than if you had waited for them to discover your mistake for themselves. Just as the longer you put off going to the dentist, the more your tooth will ache, you have every interest in ridding yourself as soon as possible of remorse for an act of which you are not very proud.

Do not expect your husband to apologize to you all day long because he knows once and for all that smoking bothers you but that you will open the window as soon as his back is turned, and that watching football matches on television bores you to death but that you will take advantage of the time to catch up on your phone calls in the next room; he also knows very well that he pulls most of the blanket to his side of the bed, that dawn finds you shivering and uncovered and that twin beds would be much more practical than all the apologies he could offer. But if you spill soup on his shoulder, strike his finger with a hammer, or simply step on his toes, you should know that apologies of the type one makes in the underground will be quite inadequate and that you will have to pamper and comfort him with as much zeal and anguish as if he were your little son and had just fallen out of the window.

APPETITE

While hunger is physiological, appetite is intellectual. Although my dog may turn up his nose at his ordinary meal, he will rush drooling in advance at the sight of a piece of chocolate, and husbands and children are no different from him in this respect.

Presentation, novelty, publicity ('I've made something you love for dinner'), and curiosity ('Close your eyes, I have a surprise for you') will do more to excite your husband's appetite than even the most perfectly prepared dish that he is in the habit of eating every other day.

And I am afraid that the same is true of your personal charms. Habit is the worst enemy of happy marriages. (See also Dinner)

APPROVAL

If you always say 'yes' and endorse all the decisions of your father, your husband, your boss or your son, in order to live in peace, don't be surprised when they no longer bother to ask you for advice.

Where your father is concerned, I don't think that it is necessary to encourage you to revolt, because parents only have to express an idea for their children immediately to support the opposite opinion. And I wonder if the best educational method would not be to impose upon children exactly the contrary of what we wish them to do.

But I hope for your sake, madame, that your husband consults you on all the important decisions of your life and that you take the trouble to discuss them with him, for otherwise you will deprive him of the great joy of having to convince you. Even in politics, dyed-in-the-wool partisans haven't a terribly good reputation, and to be called a 'yes-man' has never been considered a compliment.

However, systematically criticizing all your boss's ideas will not make you very popular with him either. After all, if your employer pays you the compliment of asking for your advice, it means that he is perhaps not absolutely sure that his decision is the right one. So start by telling him that his idea is marvellous and that you would never have been able to think of such a good one (even if at first view it strikes you as stupid), but

. . . isn't he afraid that this or that little drawback may perhaps cause his brilliant plan to fail, etc. . . . If the change is good for the company but entails additional work for you, don't try to sabotage it but ask for a raise, reminding yourself that if your boss has tried to give you the impression that he is seeking your advice, it is simply in order to make the pill go down easier, and he will be grateful to you if you swallow it without making a bad face.

(See also Criticism)

ARROGANCE

Beware of those men who cannot resist making scornful and sarcastic remarks. They may be witty, but they are also cruel, and the day will come when they will spare you no more than everybody else.

(See also Snobs)

ARTISTS

An artist is a man who has a passion for his work and for life in general, who cultivates an obsession, a talent or a hobby that fascinates him, knowing that any activity can become an art if it is performed with love. The world's best guarantee of happiness is to marry a man who is an artist in the broadest sense of the term, provided that you are prepared to share his enthusiasm.

Moreover, nothing prevents you, mesdames, from

becoming artists in your own work, in your gardening, your cooking, and even in bed, and from leading the 'life of an artist' within yourself.

In short, being an artist means being able to transform the bitter brew of the most ungrateful tasks into an intoxicating honey, and the grey dust of everyday life into pink champagne.

ATHLETES

Ever since the days of ancient Greece, athletes have been considered demigods, and their biceps often bring them more money and success than a Cambridge honours degree. People are always a little distrustful of an intellectual, never of a great sportsman. There is, however, a whole category of sportsmen who are difficult to live with if you haven't exactly the same tastes and abilities as they. The frontier separating the pleasant, relaxed, contented sportsmen from the fanatics is situated exactly halfway between those who enjoy indulging in outdoor exercise and those who want to win a medal. It is possible to live with the first, but you are a slave to the competitions of the second. To take just one example from among all the different sports: there is nothing more heady and romantic than a promenade for two on skis over the virgin snow away from the beaten track, taking time to admire the extraordinary beauty and silence of the landscape and stopping to share a sandwich on a tree trunk in the sunshine. And nothing is more boring than to ski down the same icy track ten times in succession in the midst of a noisy crowd in order to improve one's time by a few tenths of a second. As for walking, will you please tell me what pleasure remains when a stroll becomes a marathon?

But to return to our daily life and to the place that athletes can hold in it, it is certain that you must be able to keep up with the sporting abilities of your husband if you want to share his leisure pastimes and his pleasure, and that you should never marry a camper if you suffer from hay fever.

It seems to me that a lady champion who falls in love with a boy who has no talent for sports should love him enough to forget her own records if she does not want to end up in last place in the race for happiness.

There also exists another category of athletes – less risky but slightly comical: the armchair athletes, champions of television-watching. They obviously prevent you from seeing the programme that interests you, but you need only emit a grunt every fifteen minutes or so in order to give the impression that you are following the event with breathless interest.

Needless to say, all this advice is addressed exclusively to women who, like me, are bored to death by Sports with a capital S.

ATTRACTION

The wave of attraction that instinctively brings two people together more often resembles love at first sight than does true friendship, which is slow to develop; but, like love at first sight, it can vanish just as suddenly when the two people get to know each other a little better. Some people attract others without being at all worthy of their response, while others have forbidding exteriors and hearts of gold.

Being attractive to others is a gift that owes much to physical appearance – and for once fat is more appealing than skin and bones – but, like elegance, it can be acquired. A ready smile, a direct look, a firm handshake, a clear and confident voice are all means of attracting friends – as political candidates are well aware!

One might say that all human relations are based on the attraction or antipathy that one inspires, and if there is one thing in the world worth cultivating, it is certainly this particular form of charm.

In a crowd, on a bus or at a cocktail party, the sight of a man who is a total stranger to you rings a bell in your ears, your pulse accelerates, and your stomach feels hollow. It is perhaps the beginning of a great love, but for the moment it is neither more nor less than an irresistible desire for a bar of chocolate, a pair of shoes, or an antique displayed in a shop-window. Furthermore, once you know him well, the man in question may produce the same sort of results as those three objects:

Almost before you have swallowed it, you know that tomorrow morning you will curse that piece of chocolate as you watch the needle of the bathroom scales leap forward . . . just as you will regret having gone out with the handsome stranger who, like certain cities which are so lovely seen from an aeroplane and so sordid when you visit them on foot, may be unable to withstand closer inspection.

Practical experience soon proves that the shoes hurt you . . . and so may he.

Finally, the antique is far beyond your means and it is better to forget it. Prince Charmings who marry shepherdesses are increasingly rare, and what good will it do you, I ask you, to be attracted to the heir to an oil fortune? They populate the dreams of half the feminine population in the country, and unless you are stimulated by the sheer thrill of competition, it is much more sensible to think twice before you give in to impulses that are glandular in origin.

BACHELORS

What exactly is a bachelor? An egotist? A hero? A Don Juan? A woman-hater? A male 'old maid'? A hapless fellow who pays higher income taxes than other people? A man reduced to the meagre resources of the company canteen at lunchtime and to a lonely fried egg for dinner? A habitué of the lowest fashionable night-club? A free man? A bachelor may be a little of all these things, but in any case he is a man who is encountered with increasing rarity in this age of early marriage and easy divorce.

But a man who chooses to remain single is a living reproach to the majority of those who have married, even when the latter are relatively content with their lot. A bachelor is a non-conformist, an individualist, who treats himself to a convertible car instead of a washing-machine and to dinner in a restaurant instead of a baby-sitter. He is a man whom all the hostesses fight over and who kindles a gleam of interest in the eyes of all the girls. In short, he is the personification of regret for lost freedom – Public Enemy Number One, who must be eliminated by marrying him off as soon as possible. In order to be convinced of this state of affairs, you need only observe the boisterous (because unforced) jubilation of the guests at a bachelor's dinner on the eve of his wedding. Had I been born a man, that alone would induce me to marry as late in life as possible!

While men look askance at one of their brethren's enjoyment of a freedom they themselves have relinquished in exchange for homely comfort, women, on the other hand, regard bachelors in quite a different light. If they are already married, a bachelor is someone who is always prepared to accept a last-minute dinner invitation and he also has the free time and the funds to take them to a concert (which George detests) or to the films on the evenings when the poor darling is poring over his income tax return or the company's Annual Report. If they are bachelor girls themselves, they are prepared to go to any lengths in order to change this mutual state of affairs by steering men imperceptibly from the role of bachelor into that of fiancé. In which event there are two possibilities: either the women are stronger than the men, and the bachelors will end up as husbands; or the reverse is true and the bachelors will escape. Some men may think they have managed to reconcile their freedom with their comfort by remaining attached for years to the same mistress, but they merely succeed in giving the world a flagrant demonstration of the immensity of masculine egotism.

In any case, women adore bachelors, for by refraining

from singling out any individual woman as a wife, they pay homage to all the others. So when this rare bird decides to marry at the age of forty or fifty, all his charming girl-friends are rather cool in their congratulations, and after one or two dinner parties in order to cast a critical eye on the creature who robbed them of their knight and escort, they decide that the new couple really isn't the least bit interesting. The husband, who innocently rejoiced at the idea that his friend Paul was finally going to enjoy the matrimonial chains of a well-heated doghouse with meals at regular hours after all the risks and perils of his bachelor adventures, is surprised at the end of a few weeks not to see him come round so often. Let him observe the faraway look and the tight-lipped expression on his wife's face. Even the most faithful of wives cannot bear to be betrayed by 'her' personal bachelor.

Unmarried women used to be either old maids or unwed mothers; today they are bachelors just like unmarried men, and for an ever increasing number of them it has become a question of choice rather than of fate. There is no reason why it should be otherwise, since they have the same careers, the same responsibilities, the same pay, and the freedom to bear children only when they choose to do so. However, they are a long way from enjoying the popularity of their masculine counterparts in the eyes of society hostesses, and they are invited less and less frequently by married couples. A bachelor girl should therefore resign herself to being ill considered in hotels and restaurants, to leading not too conventional a life, and to frequenting single rather than married people.

The conception of single women as bachelors, perfectly adult and in no way inferior to men, is the greatest innovation of our age.

(See also Homosexuals)

BALL GAMES

Although I haven't any actual statistics at hand, I suppose that at least half the feminine population is just as interested in football, rugby and cricket matches as are their husbands, brothers, fathers and the other men in their lives. And so I will address myself only to the remaining half who consider that a ball, whether it be round or oval, is a dangerous object that hurts a lot when it hits you in the face. This category of women, to which I myself belong, should nevertheless participate in one way or another in the activity that so absorbs their husbands. It isn't really very difficult to remember the names of one or two famous players, or to know that Wales beat France, or vice versa. Finally, instead of regretting the hours you might have spent together hand in hand as in your youth, you should be realistic and realize that the only thing that is absolutely unbearable after a certain number of years of married life is for one partner to be interested only in his mate, in what he or she says, thinks and does, to the exclusion of everything else.

The ideal solution is, of course, for a couple to share the same tastes and the same interests. But it is still better to have a husband who is mad about a sport that bores you, than a husband who isn't interested in anything at all.

BARMEN

When a respectable woman reaches the point of telling the story of her life to a barman she must really be very lonely. On the other hand, few men have not had in their lives a barman who served them optimism along with their whisky, and who listened to their sad tales with a professionally sympathetic ear. A barman, in short, is a sort of minute medicine-man, and while he dispenses the same oblivion as does a bottle of whisky drained in solitude, he spikes it with an inestimable ingredient: sympathy. There is a most extraordinary complicity and masculine understanding between a barman and his regular customers, and their mutual confidence is such that very often the barman becomes a moneylender and even a little bit of a procurer. His is a profession that certainly requires, for success, more psychology than actual talent for mixing drinks.

And so, mesdames, you ought to forgive the men in your life if they have sought refuge in a bar, and try to find out why. If you have given them the human warmth they crave, they will probably be less likely to seek it in alcohol.

BATHROOMS

A bathroom can be the death-chamber of love. If, instead of encouraging pre-marital relations in bed, we delivered marriage certificates only to couples who had shared the same bathroom for a week, many a divorce would be avoided.

Whenever you wonder about the temperature of your love for your husband, take a look at the bathroom – it is the Delphic oracle of modern times.

Passionate Love: 'Oh, look, he used my toothbrush, the absent-minded darling. And all that water and the soap on the floor and these soaking towels – how manly he is!'

Lukewarm Love: 'I simply must buy him a toothbrush in a different colour from mine. It's intolerable the way he always mistakes them! And all that water, and the towels that were changed just this morning – if only we could each have our own bathroom!'

Love Grown Cold: 'The swine, *my* toothbrush! It's disgusting! And the water, the soap, these towels – he treats me like a maid. Oh, for hotel life and independence!'

It is certain that in one marriage out of two the husband never puts the top back on the toothpaste tube, or else he squeezes it in the middle, and I think you will admit that it is irritating to have to crawl about on all fours every morning looking for a missing toothpaste cap.

In order to avoid any possible disputes and irritation, here are a few tips:

Have two different medicine cupboards, or at least two separate shelves, two glasses that are easily identified (you can buy charming ones labelled 'His' and 'Hers') and two tubes of toothpaste and so on. And when you are rich, have two bedrooms and two bathrooms. It's so much more civilized!

BEARDS

Show me your beard and I will tell you who you are!

Infatuated with his own image but at the same time less sure of himself than he appears to be, the very young man, suffering from his all too evident adolescence, who lovingly brushes the first signs of a beard around his chin, says to himself every morning as he gazes into his mirror: 'What a handsome intellectual air you have, my boy!'

But within the limits of the fashion at the time, beards and moustaches can amazingly improve a face that would be banal without them. A weak chin or a double one is no longer noticeable when it is masked by a beard, and a large nose seems much less prominent when a moustache fills in the excessively wide space that may separate it from the upper lip. You will also be less apt to notice that a man's lips are too thick or too thin if they are surrounded by a growth of hair. It should be unnecessary to add that if a man indulges in the luxury of such fancies – which, it must be admitted, denote a certain degree of conceit – his beard or moustache should at least be impeccably trimmed, brushed and even lightly perfumed, just as a smooth-shaven man should never be seen with more than a twelve-hour growth of stubble.

Growing a beard or a moustache can also be a distraction and a diversion or, on the contrary, the renunciation of all effort. A bearded invalid looks even more ill and a freshly shaven tramp is no longer a tramp. Furthermore, when a man is not feeling well the first thing he does is to stop shaving, just as the woman who is feeling depressed no longer bothers to make up.

Finally, a twelve-hour growth of beard has the effect of a rasp on a woman's fragile skin, and the most elementary courtesy on the part of a gentleman who wishes to kiss a lady is not to martyrize her. He must therefore remember to shave before dashing off to his rendezvous – or to shave after dinner or on returning from the office, if he wishes to prove to his wife that he is a thoughtful and considerate husband.

There is no doubt that the pilosity of a man is one of the most revealing indications of his state of mind, and I cannot advise you too strongly to observe it most attentively.

BEAU

A term that conjures up the days of *Gone With the Wind* but is still used at all ages (beyond thirteen) to refer to a male who is currently attentive but hasn't reached the fiancé stage.

(See also Boy-friends, Lovers, Suitors, Sweetheart)

BEAUTY

What exactly is masculine beauty? Above all it is a question of proportion and general allure rather than regular features.

While true beauty has a quality of timelessness, the appreciation of beauty is governed by the caprices of fashion, and sometimes when we see a picture of a man whose beauty was famous and celebrated by the writers of his time, it makes us wonder . . .

Beauty is the first thing a good fairy bestows with a wave of her wand over the cradle of a baby girl, but I wonder if beauty in a man doesn't complicate rather than facilitate his life. You seldom see very handsome men succeed in anything but the theatre or the films. Adulated by their mothers and by women, they generally become smug and self-centred, and they do not grow old gracefully.

However, the bad reputation attached to masculine beauty has disappeared. Manufacturers of beauty products of all kinds have decided that it was foolish to ignore half the consumer population, and have turned their attention to this colossal unexploited market. We have witnessed an outburst of special magazines, cosmetics, beauty salons – an entire arsenal of everything that can beautify and adorn our husbands and beaux, of whom we previously demanded only suitable size, good teeth, and, above all, brains.

BLIND DATES

Because the ultimate disgrace for a girl is to be dateless on Saturday night, she has a girl-friend ask her own date to bring along a friend; and if this new couple get along well, so much the better!

The point of a blind date is to make a good impression on a young man who is a total stranger and who hasn't even had an opportunity to feel for you that first attraction which might have inspired him to ask you for a date himself.

There are two possible eventualities. In the first, the young man turns out to be physically repulsive to you and the idea that he might hold you in his arms gives you goose-flesh. The best solution is to say to yourself that it is only a brief unpleasant moment to be endured and, keeping your distance, try to be a good sport and make the best of it, especially so as not to offend your friend's beau, who, after all, has tried to do you a favour and who may be able to come up with something better the next time. Since you haven't the slightest desire to make a conquest, you can take advantage of the chance to talk a lot, be witty and overwhelm him with your superiority. It is better for the boy in question to tell everyone you are an impossible snob than that you are a sulky idiot; it might even intrigue some of the young men who come into the second category – blind dates whom you find attractive.

The latter will be pleasantly surprised to find – instead of the parrot they were prepared to pluck – a tender dove, all ears, honey and cooing. But take care not to overdo it. Unless he is an utter imbecile, every modern young man is perfectly familiar with your little tricks and it is not enough to bat your eyelashes with a rapturous air in order to convince him that you are listening heart and soul to his epic account of the third goal scored by Spurs last Saturday.

According to a survey among brilliant college students (because it is a brilliant young man you want, isn't it?), this is what they seek in a girl:

First of all, naturalness. It is impossible to play a role all one's life and the only means of holding on to a man for a long time is to be yourself. Besides, how can you guess what kind of a person will appeal to somebody you haven't even met yet? And even if you know that this stranger has gone out a lot with a tall, ethereal blonde who is an expert in yoga, how can you be sure that he isn't completely fed up with the 'lotus' and that the girl who will win him forever won't be a plump little brunette who knows twenty different recipes for apple pie? Remember that you may perhaps get away with an act for one evening, but that a permanent lack of naturalness leads straight to a nervous breakdown.

Next, they want to be taken seriously by a person as

intelligent as themselves. Since you have heard over and over again that men hate intelligent women, instead of talking to them about the paper you have just written on Hindu philosophy, you generally launch into a recital of the latest gossip to excite your little set and, since it concerns people he doesn't even know, it bores him to death. The best technique is to send out feelers on such subjects as politics, psychology, films, books, etc., and see which one sparks his interest. As soon as you have discovered the key that unlocks his reservoir of eloquence, settle back comfortably and let him talk. Only when we are young do we take the time to explain our views, and these all-night discussions are more enriching than any course by any professor. The day when you no longer feel like exchanging general ideas is the day when you will start to be old.

It seems that there are more and more young men who ask point-blank at the end of half an hour, 'Will you go all the way?' and if the answer is 'No', they disappear. There is nothing new in this behaviour, except that its modern form is singularly lacking in subtlety. There are certainly still many girls who reply 'No', when they would perhaps have wanted nothing more than to let themselves go if they hadn't had to make the decision themselves, and I think that you aren't losing very much in letting these lazy seducers walk out of your life.

When making love requires no more reflection and desire than eating a ham sandwich, it won't give any greater pleasure either.

BLOOD PRESSURE

Every day we hear about people suddenly dropping dead, and the sleepless nights of many a businessman are haunted by fears of a heart attack.

It is within your power to expel this nightmare from your husband's dreams. You can get him used to eating less and less salt, and finally banish the salt-cellar from the table forever, because he often reaches for it without thinking. You can serve dinner before he has had time to pour himself a second martini. You can also try to choose the most propitious moment for announcing unpleasant news, instead of assailing him practically the moment you hear his key in the front door. Avoid quarrels, which are always futile, and if he hasn't much appetite in bed, don't wear him out by forcing your attentions on him.

Although men may be stronger than we are, they are also more fragile and less able to take care of themselves, and marriage is simply a sort of mutual protection society.

BOREDOM

Here is the great enemy, the intellectual cancer, the evil adviser, the most effective destructive weapon, the reef on which almost all unsuccessful marriages are shipwrecked. It is partly from boredom that girls have affairs with boys at an even earlier age and literally pursue them with their attentions. It is from boredom that people marry more and more quickly and divorce just as fast. It is from boredom that women surround themselves with an ever-increasing brood of children, and from boredom that they then feel like running away from it all. It is from boredom that men drink and young people take drugs. It is from boredom that the new dances have become what they are – voodoo rites. It is in order to kill their boredom that people kill themselves with work and find it impossible to relax. It is boredom that occupies psychiatrists' couches and rehab clinics.

Heaven knows, however, that almost all the inventions of the past fifty years have conspired to eliminate this insidious evil: from cars to television, from paid holidays to foreign travel, from sensational magazines to sex education – everything, absolutely everything, has been organized to amuse people, and the result is that never in history have people been so bored, because they have lost the habit of finding their amusements for themselves. They need lots of noise and more and more friends in order not to feel lonely. They also need to indulge in a fever of activity, and retirement is perhaps the number one incurable malady of the century, for it probably kills even more men than cars do.

I cannot offer an explanation for this phenomenon, because I myself am never bored – which may be simply a gift of nature like my curly hair. But I suppose that I have also made an effort – and perhaps you can do the same.

Disregarding all advice, I chose as a husband a boy

with whom I had fun; yes, that was really the principal reason for my marriage, and I have never regretted it. I have pitilessly dropped all boring people; I taught my daughter to laugh; I have always refused to read depressing, fashionable novels, and I've switched off the radio programmes that didn't please me, even though it may be unseemly not to like Schoenberg; and after one month of lessons I stopped trying to hit golf balls because I simply wasn't interested in the game.

But I have watched birds fly and clouds sail across the skies, and I have let the sun wrap me in its soft blanket; I have seen plants grow, fade and die, gathering the seeds to be planted the following year, and I have also gathered fruit to make into preserves for the winter; in other words, I have made plans and I have put forth the necessary effort to accomplish them. In short, I always try to know what I like and I am willing to work as hard as necessary in order to obtain it. If I had remained in my armchair twiddling my thumbs, today I would be like nine people out of ten: bored to tears. But I believe firmly in the proverb: 'Heaven helps those who help themselves'.

(See also Yawns)

BOSS

It is almost as important to have a good boss as it is to have a good husband, and here is my portrait of an ideal one.

First of all, he should have a pleasing appearance. I realize that a man can be an excellent employer without being an Adonis; but in this case he must possess great strength of character and radiate intelligence to compensate for his poor features or undistinguished physique.

Handsome or not, the primordial quality of a good boss is authority.

Authority is like chic: you have it or you don't. Just like certain women who, mistaking astonishment for admiration, confuse eccentricity with elegance, certain men, impressed by the army sergeants of their youth, think they have to bark in order to be obeyed. They are usually men who suffer from timidity but refuse to face the fact, and they remind me of a piece of second-rate meat covered with a very hot curry sauce. Others have so little self-confidence that they think if they so much as smile at an employee, the latter will immediately pat them on the back, and so they wear in all circumstances the expression of an undertaker who has swallowed a truncheon.

A good boss should also have a very well-developed social conscience and, while his first concern should be the prosperity of his business, his second should be the welfare of his employees. After all, just as machines need to be oiled in order to function properly, human beings work well only if they are treated with consideration, and the policy of the kick in the a— is completely obsolete.

Needless to say, an ideal boss is never lazy; in fact,

in order to win the esteem of his employees, he should work a little more than they do.

Finally, he should be lucky, boldly enterprising, and he should therefore keep up to date with all the latest techniques.

He should know how to render justice, to be a good speaker and writer. While he ought to know how to do everything better than any of his employees, he should also be able to select his collaborators with such discernment that he can have complete confidence in them. A boss is like an orchestra conductor directing a symphony. He is the only one who is familiar with the complete score. And a man who wants to verify every tiny detail can never be a real leader.

(See also Job)

BOY-FRIENDS

To have a man for a good friend is a blessing from heaven. But in order to merit masculine friendship, you have to go to even more trouble than it takes to hold on to a lover.

A young girl meets all sorts of boys. Some of them become boy-friends and others simply friends, but these roles are not distributed in advance by fate – it is often a question of timing. In all cases, there must be a wave of mutual appreciation, of similar ideas and the same sense of humour, for it is certainly easier to win a friend by laughter than by tears. If, when they meet, each one is in love with somebody else, the friendship will take form at once and it will be years before either of them imagines that the status of friend might possibly develop into something more romantic. But in order to establish a feeling of complete confidence between a boy and a girl, you must be tactful and never rush things. In fact, a girl who is too flirtatious, too demanding, or too much of an 'outraged princess', will probably never know the joy of having a man for a friend, because she will always hope to turn him into a new slave. Furthermore, some young women feel humiliated if a man resists their charms, and they run to the beauty salon or to the dentist to make sure that they still have 'white teeth and sweet breath'.

If at the end of a few years there is no joy or pain or even humiliation that you don't want to confide immediately to this man who holds a special place in your life, and if he too finds in you an indefatigably willing ear and a faithful but clairvoyant ally, you can be sure that you have a real friend.

Sometimes you run the risk of losing him when you get married, because new husbands are always jealous of this exceptional relationship. You even see husbands who are jealous of their wives' best girl-friends, and wives who resent their husband's close friendship with his 'pals'. Neither should you hope to find many true friends towards the end of your life, because hearts dry out just like complexions, and one must be very young in heart in order to be interested in other people.

(See also Beau, Lovers, Suitors, Sweetheart)

BREASTS

I have always wondered whether the adoration men display for bountiful breasts is not merely due to a subconscious recollection of being well fed. Has anyone ever thought of making a survey to find out if the majority of homosexuals were not bottle-fed babies?

BROTHERS

A brother can be the most generous and least demanding man in your life, whereas a father has the right to insist on respect and obedience and always feels a certain possessiveness toward his daughter.

There are two kinds of brothers: big ones and little ones.

A big brother, an older one, sometimes tends to consider himself a second father, to look after his little sister and to exercise over her an authority that he has not yet acquired outside the family. As soon as his sister starts going out with boys, he wants to meet her friends and is sometimes even more concerned about her honour than are her parents. In the Mediterranean regions, a man who kills the seducer of his sister is automatically acquitted. If you have such a tyrannical brother, you should realize that if you let him get away with it you will slip into the habit of being martyrized by all men. Tell him firmly that he needn't supervise you so closely. Your father will surely be more lenient, and he is the only person to whom you can turn for moral support. If your brother is really excessively domineering, perhaps he isn't exactly perfect either, and this is the ideal situation in which to practise a little friendly blackmail.

Fortunately an elder brother is more often a marvellous friend than a watchdog, and a girl who has always been surrounded by boys is less surprised by her first love affair as well as less vulnerable. Furthermore, an elder brother introduces her to his friends, excluding those in whom he hasn't complete confidence. He is her first party escort, her first tennis partner, her maths tutor, her favourite confidant, and often her ambassador to the family matriarch, who is always unable to resist a request from her beloved son. Later, alas, this beautiful relationship can come to an end with the arrival on the scene of a sister-in-law. But if I had known the joy of having an elder brother, I think that I would have been able to take an awful lot from her in order to preserve this unique relationship, which is one of the closest that a woman can ever have with a man.

A little brother, a younger one, can be either a heavy burden or a marvellous toy, depending on the intensity of your maternal instincts. But don't let yourself be fooled. Quite soon, this marvellous toy is going to stop working, for even before he has learned how to talk he will know whether you are his slave or his enemy. In the first case, he will exploit you to the maximum, because an older sister has always been men's favourite servant. On the other hand, if he knows that you will not yield to his caprices, he will play the meanest tricks on you. A little boy always starts by hating 'girls', and he will ridicule you with that gang of monsters that he calls his pals. But everything will straighten out later on, as soon as he has become sensitive to feminine charm, and he will then be grateful to you for having been firm with him and for having made him wash behind his ears.

Big or little, a brother is above all a man, and knowing how to make him love you is ideal training for learning how to charm all the other men who are to come in your life.

BRUSH-OFF

There are usually more men in your life that you would like to get rid of than there are Prince Charmings whom you are dying to meet. How should you deal with the door-to-door salesman, the insurance agent, the college student selling magazine subscriptions, the moustached nun or the fund-raiser for the Society for Suppressing Cancer in Pigeons, who knock on your door? You can slam it in their faces, which would be the safest thing to do but not very kindly, because the job of door-to-door selling is often a last resort; or you can let the person enter and find yourself a few minutes later the owner of six dozen coloured pencils in the best of cases, or tied to a chair, robbed of your life savings in the worst. Never thoughtlessly open your door to anybody, and never hesitate to ask who is there when you are not expecting a caller, or else equip your front door with a one-way spy hole.

It is easier to get rid of strangers to whom you owe nothing than bores who have been duly introduced to you. If a man you met the night before and who made the worst impression on you loses no time in telephoning you the very next morning, be as busy as possible: you're just about to leave on a trip, your mother or your children have the 'flu, you're cramming for an exam, you're writing a book – think of any excuse at all. If you don't mind being impolite, you can even say that you have to write a letter or take the dog for a walk.

Then there is the case of the man who interested you for a while and to whom you accorded your favours. The only thing you can now reproach him for is loving you too much. It will be very difficult to get him to regress from a privileged position in your life to that of a casual acquaintance. But if your interest in him has waned to the point where you don't care if he becomes an enemy, tell him that you don't like his face any more and to go to the devil – that should do it. If you prefer to be more subtle and to protect his masculine vanity, you must manage to make him think that it was he who took the initiative in breaking off relations. In order to lead him to the breaking point, you can:

– greet him with your hair in curlers and your face covered with cream, preferably green.

– arrive at a rendezvous two hours late.

– cancel a date at the very last minute, after having

made him queue up all morning to get tickets for the opera.

– bring along two very ugly visiting girl-friends to a dinner that he hoped would be intimate, in a restaurant that is beyond his means.

– swear like a trooper in front of his parents.

– get drunk, if he never touches a drop.

– tell him that you want to have at least six children and ask him what are his favourite names, if you know that he isn't interested in getting married.

– describe in gruesome detail your most intimate maladies.

– let tears well up in your eyes at the most harmless remark, or assume the martyrized expression of a person who is suffering in silence.

But if by chance he bears up under this treatment, you ought to think twice – because you are unlikely to find another man so very much in love with you.

BUDGET

Mademoiselle, it is probable that while you were a young girl living with your parents you lightheartedly spent all your pocket-money as fancy struck you. Later on, when you got a job, your greatest financial problem was to figure out how long it would take to save up enough money to buy that divine little Chanel suit if you cut out desserts. But when you leave home for good, and your young husband shares his earnings with you, your problems are going to become much more complicated, and I hope that you will have learned how to handle them fairly well when you have to stretch your budget to provide for a baby too.

Your husband already has enough trouble simply earning an adequate salary. It's up to you to spend it in the most advantageous way. As soon as you have calculated your normal weekly expenses, you should make a budget for the entire year. Take a large sheet of paper and divide it into columns headed: Food, Clothing, Upkeep, Car or Transport, Pleasure, etc. – and I would be very surprised if, after adding up the total, your hair doesn't stand on end!

CARESSES

Oh, what a lovely word, evocative of more or less forbidden pleasures! There are all sorts of caresses, from those you distractedly give to a tail-wagging puppy, to the ones that have been carefully studied like the rites of some sacred dance.

Sentimentally speaking, caresses are of value only when they are spontaneous and not performed like a well-learned lesson. But it would be deliberately closing one's eyes to certain aspects of the masculine nature not to admit that many women hold on to their husbands and lovers primarily by means of artful caresses. As for women, the more deeply we're in love, the less we feel the need for skilled caresses; the hand of the man we love on our shoulders is far more effective than fantastic feats of gymnastics learned in the embrace of professionals.

Some women must be thrilled by the precise, bold gesture of a stranger in a crowd, for if they weren't, it would be hard to understand why these satyrs should continue – but I must say that I don't know a single woman who has ever been willing to admit it. I suppose that women, unlike men, are a little bit ashamed if they enjoy technique for its own sake.

CARS

A car is the favourite toy of men of all ages, but their taste changes with the years and the motor show could very well arrange the different stands as in a department store, with a children's shop, a teen-age section, a boutique for twenty-year-olds – and older. As soon as a young man has been able to buy (or to persuade Dad to give him) his first real car, the one that comes right after the miniature cars of his childhood, he looks after it as if it were a mistress. (As a matter of fact, in French, and even in English, a car is feminine in gender.) While he will happily let an entire month go by without bothering to make his bed, he will spend hours polishing 'her' chrome with some very expensive product, and every Saturday he will made an expedition to a car-accessory shop to see what new offering he can made to his idol. As with a mistress, he tires of her rather quickly, and each year the opening of the motor show marks the end of his fidelity and enthusiasm. His imagination is set aflame with such magic words as fuel injection and disc brakes, all of which are utterly unintelligible to a woman.

Fortunately for the car companies, women buy cars too, and, convinced that in this day and age any car will run if you simply put a little petrol in the tank and a little oil in the motor, they base their choice entirely on the style of the chassis and the colour of the upholstery. But a car never occupies the same place in their lives as it does in the life of a man, because a man loves his car not only for itself but also for its power to increase his self-esteem. Formerly, a man of rank was immediately recognizable by his clothing, his retinue of servants and the family crest painted on his carriage door. But today, practically the only thing that differentiates a rich man from a country bumpkin at first glance is the make of his car, and the silver lady on the Rolls-Royce bonnet has taken the place of the coats of arms of yesteryear.

However, a woman who is naïve enough to believe in the image that men try to give of themselves by means of their cars runs the risk of being somewhat disillusioned when she gets to know them better, and it is time she learned to see through the smokescreen behind which our modern centaurs like to hide.

In France, the driver of a 2 CV Citroën might be a student with his first car, an elderly labourer who bought it secondhand, a house painter who uses it to cart his ladders around, a famous interior decorator delivering a signed antique commode or a gentleman farmer who uses it to inspect his land.

The driver of a Peugeot or of a black DS may be the director of a big corporation who doesn't want the trade union to be able to say that the boss bought himself a Mercedes with the profits that should have been spent on a raise for the workers; or he may be the chauffeur of the above corporation director who has carefully hidden his cap under the seat, the corner grocer or a small-town lawyer.

The driver of a Rolls or a Bentley could be a rock star, the latest fashionable designer or hairdresser, an Englishman or possibly a grocer.

Certain details are also eloquent: shields from foreign countries, stuffed animals in the window or lucky charms hanging from the rear-view mirror show that the owner is much too unsophisticated to have been rich for very long.

Finally, a man's style of driving is most revealing. Does he keep to the left like a good boy, and does he automatically find himself in the longest line of cars, and does he always need to be reminded that the light is green? If so, he is a calm type of person who will provide you with a future devoid of surprises, but also devoid of drama, and with a little luck you will end your days in Nice, strolling hand in hand along the Promenade des Anglais.

Or, on the other hand, does he accelerate when the lights turn yellow in order to beat the red light? Does he constantly change from one lane to another? Does he swear at other drivers? If so, he is highstrung and overworked – the most common type of man at the moment – desperately rushing to go nowhere in particular, and he is a promising candidate for a nervous breakdown.

Is he forever making sweeping gestures, as he controls the steering-wheel with his little finger? He is a dangerous exhibitionist. Does he cut in front of other cars, or speed up as soon as anybody tries to pass him? He is suffering from an inferiority complex. And finally, does he consider his car to be a sort of annex to his bedroom? Beware, the palace he describes to you is perhaps no more than an attic flat that he shares with his ailing old mother.

Women must really be very unobservant, or else they enjoy being taken in, to be unable immediately to analyse a man's character as soon as he sits behind a steering-wheel; and men who are determined to keep their characters or activities secret are advised to become pedestrians or bus riders.

When the man of your life offers to take you for a ride in his car, it is a little as if he were presenting you to his family, and you mustn't underestimate the importance of the occasion. The gentlest man in the world can become a tiger when he drives, and although that makes two of them when you take into account the one that is already in his tank, this isn't the moment to act like a trainer with a whip, but rather like a silent and devoted secretary. Remember that you are bound to irritate a man, no matter how much he likes you, if you

– use the rear-view mirror to repair your make-up;
– leave personal objects in the glove compartment;
– tell him that the light is green;

– misread the map he gave you and tell him to turn to the left when you meant to say 'to the right';

– exclaim, when he makes a mistake, 'I told you so!'

– ask him to stop every twenty-five miles so that you can 'wash your hands';

– put your arms around his neck while taking a hair-pin turn on a mountain road, or for that matter even on a motorway;

– scream delightedly when you spot a new-born lamb in an adjacent pasture;

– become ridiculously panicky as soon as he goes faster than thirty-five miles an hour, and desperately step on imaginary brakes;

– offer to help him if the car breaks down;

– do *not* offer to help him if the car breaks down;

– play with the radio, unless he has asked you to find a good programme;

– launch into a deep philosophical conversation – or, in fact, any conversation requiring more than a grunt for a reply;

– tell him, when driving in the city, that he went past twenty wonderful parking-places without seeing them and that now you will have to walk for half an hour in the rain;

– don't call all the drivers who pass you crazy, admire bigger cars and fail to criticize the upkeep of cars that are just the same model as his;

– remain seated, waiting for him to open your door

(he will probably have reached the corner before he realizes that you are still waiting in the car).

Let's suppose that you have been simply perfect and that your escort wishes to prove how much he likes you in rather too obvious a manner by transforming the innocent car seat into a double bed. Unless you happen to enjoy this form of exercise, it is always a good idea to practise discretely opening the door beforehand, because many men sober up rapidly in the fresh air. Remember that one-third of all illegitimate babies are conceived in these particular circumstances.

If your car breaks down when you are driving alone, it is very seldom that a sympathetic, mechanically minded male, spotting a woman on the verge of tears beside an opened bonnet, will not stop to offer his assistance. Accept it gracefully, but at the slightest suggestion of payment in kind, display the blackest ingratitude or offer him some cash.

Finally, if you want to hang on to your jewels, not to mention your life, never stop to pick up hitch-hikers, even if they are angelic-looking nuns. Who knows? Their long robes may conceal hairy male legs, their wimples a stubble of beard, and there may be a Luger hidden up their sleeves.

(See also Drivers)

CHARM

Charm means magic. Otherwise, how can you explain the fact that a woman can fall in love at first sight with a bean-pole of a man with thinning hair? Charm is far from being reserved for women alone. Cities, houses, landscapes, objects and animals can all be charming – so why not men?

It is generally true that a foreigner has more charm than a compatriot, because one of the ingredients of charm is mystery. Charm has nothing to do with beauty or elegance, but it still depends on a certain air, a voice, gestures, and especially a way of looking at you. Charm is like a perfume diffused by the soul, a subtle wave that hits you like a punch in the pit of the stomach without your knowing how or why.

A man must possess charm in order to succeed in life, whether he is a singer, an actor, or a politician; and life would be very dull indeed with a husband who is totally lacking in it.

CHEQUE-BOOK

If your husband has opened a joint account with you, it means that he has confidence in you and it would be foolish to abuse it. In order to avoid disagreeable surprises or sordid quarrels, it would be advisable to tell him you are planning to write a cheque to pay for some specific purchase.
(See also Budget)

CHEERFULNESS

More important even than knowing how to make boiled eggs and love, a woman should know how to be cheerful; it can completely erase the memory of a burnt joint or even a night of indifference in bed.

Remember that your husband's office staff are paid to smile, and if he finds only doleful faces at home he may be tempted to start working overtime.

Often a person doesn't become aware of the congenital bad humour of his mate until it is already too late. Instead of suffering in silence, I think that it is preferable to have a serious talk and to say that you cannot stand the sight of that gloomy face much longer. If I had a husband who was always in a bad mood, he wouldn't see me around very often.

If I were asked to classify all our human qualities in order of importance, I would give the first place to cheerfulness.

CHIC

For men as for women, chic is an inborn talent. But what are the qualities that contribute to it?

It doesn't require money. A peasant in his corduroy trousers can possess a great deal of chic, while a millionaire dressed by the finest tailor may be completely devoid of it.

It doesn't require intelligence. Contrary to charm, a

man may be chic and yet quite stupid, because chic is above all a certain air, a relaxed manner of wearing clothes as if they didn't exist.

It doesn't require beauty. A man can be ugly and chic.

Could it be simply a question of ease? I don't know if the ease is the result of chic, or chic the result of ease; but it is certain that the two go hand in hand and that the word which best defines masculine chic is 'nonchalance'.

CHORES

It must be admitted that household chores are multiplied by far more than two when you progress from bachelorhood to matrimony. It is therefore only natural for each partner to do his share.

CLUBS

Clubs are more or less exclusive places which generally admit within their walls only members of one sex; and this, it seems, is what is responsible for their appeal. The second attraction of a club is the impression you have of being part of an élite.

Your husband is therefore very proud of belonging to the Jockey Club or the local Association of Eel Fishermen, and he also knows that you will not be able to come and surprise him there. Thus both his snobbishness and desire for tranquillity are satisfied.

Nevertheless, if he ends up by spending more time at his club than he does at home, you ought to examine your conscience carefully, for there is certainly something amiss. Perhaps you put away his papers or the newspapers in some secret place known only to you. Perhaps you bore him with idle gossip instead of letting him take a nap. Perhaps you turn the television to *East-Enders* instead of letting him thrill to the Spurs football match. Perhaps you let the children ride their bicycles in the hall or wave their hatchets while screaming Indian war-cries. Perhaps you make him repair the shower as soon as he gets home, without even remembering to say 'hello'. Perhaps you serve him a tasteless dinner at nine o'clock at night; or perhaps you are simply late in returning from a visit to your friend.

Husbands are like cats. You must go to a lot of trouble if you want them to stay at home.

COMFORT

Just as it is very difficult to assume a graceful posture in too comfortable a chair, people easily lapse into egotism and vulgarity when they seek too much comfort in marriage. Men or women who marry only for reasons of comfort run the risk not only of making bad mates but also of being much more unhappy than when they were single.

Madame, if you think there is no point in bothering to cook because you only like to eat salads, if your complexion satisfies you only when you have slept all night with a clay-coloured mask on your face, if you have to protect your hands by soaking them in oil and wearing gloves to bed, and if your hair is presentable only when you wear curlers during twelve hours out of every twenty-four – don't get married! If you never get up before eleven o'clock in the morning, hate a disorderly bathroom and loathe having your toothpaste tube squeezed in the middle, if you cannot stand the smell of cigars or the sight of a triangle of bread crumbs on a dining-room chair and soiled laundry tossed in a heap in the corner – don't get married! But if you dread solitude, are embarrassed to enter a restaurant all alone and afraid to go to the cinema without an escort, if the idea of filling in an income-tax return terrifies you and if your heart is bursting with tenderness and comprehension, if a sense of devotion wells up within you until it nearly chokes you – marry right away!

Monsieur, if your razor is a sacred object, which you nevertheless hate to use twice a day, if you cannot bear to have your toothpaste tube squeezed anywhere but in the middle, if a disorderly heap of useless papers is to your mind evidence of efficiency – don't get married! If you like to read the newspaper at table and if you hate to have somebody talk to you when you are watching television or driving a car – don't get married. But if you always need to feel the presence of an audience, have a person who never forgets your birthday or even the day you first met, and all the bourgeois bliss symbolized by carpet slippers – get married right away!

But if you prefer comfort above all else, you must realize that in order to make a happy marriage it is the other person's comfort you must seek, and not your own.

COMMUNICATION

There are many more men to whom one has nothing to say than the contrary, and that is what makes social life so tiring, because you do not dare remain speechless with social acquaintances; you must, in fact, talk a great deal without saying anything. But when people have been married for a certain length of time, they no longer go to the bother of 'making conversation', and silence settles forever between the two mates like a disconnected telephone-line.

There is, however, another kind of silence between happy couples, when they understand each other perfectly without having to say a word – and this is the ultimate sign of a happy marriage.

COMPLAINTS

There should be a desert island to which we could banish all the naggers, the complainers, the eternally discontent, the imaginary invalids, the prophets of doom, the acrimonious and perpetually dissatisfied persons of all kinds. They could grab each other by the lapels and describe their miseries – while the rest of humanity would live in peace.

Lifelong complaining is one of the most effective poisons for destroying love.

(See also Criticism, Reproaches)

COMPLIMENTS
(You can't catch flies with vinegar.)

If you wish to go through life surrounded by smiling faces you must know how to pay a compliment. The vile flatterer of the famous fable knew what he was doing; he had a much more pleasant life than the grumbler who never found anything nice to say and whom everybody shunned.

Advertising companies seem to recognize man's insatiable thirst for admiration, since this, together with triumphant sex, are the two motivations on which all their campaigns are based. If I were using graphic means of expression, I would picture the fastest, most perfect lift to success in life as an immense polishing brush, with compliments at every floor.

Monsieur, you have a perfect wife. She feeds you with patiently tested recipes and she anoints her body with fragrant lotions in order to increase your pleasure in bed. In return for all this you pay her no other salary than your name and a few compliments – so don't be stingy with them.

If you wish her to continue to serve you so well, tell her:

– that she looks wonderful when she returns from a

visit to the hairdresser . . . but certainly not when she has just cleaned the entire house and is dead tired. Nothing is more irritating than a compliment at the wrong time. If, for example, I have a fever of a hundred degrees and drag myself to the office, I feel like hugging the person who tells me that I really look very peaked and that I should have stayed at home in bed, but I also feel like using the little strength I have left to strangle the person who says that I seem to be in fine form.

– that her soufflé is much better than your mother's (the only thing you risk with this kind of compliment is a steady diet of soufflés).

– that you congratulate yourself every day for having married her and that you feel awfully sorry for poor Alfred, her best friend's husband, etc., etc. Try it, starting today, and you will be surprised by the results.

Madame, you have a perfect husband. Tell him that he is strong, intelligent, clever, generous, and a marvellous lover. (Even if you have not cared to make a thorough survey as to the last point and so lack standards of comparison, the more you flatter him, the greater effort he will make.)

Mademoiselle, you've just turned twenty, you're lovely, and the entire world seems to revolve around your silky tresses. Come, come, the others aren't so bad either. Even the most apparently unattractive person has some little speciality in which he excels. While waiting for the man you cannot live without (who will perhaps be quite the opposite of what you most appreciate today), take advantage of the talents of all the others. If Harry's only attraction is his Jaguar, take him to the country where you will join up with Bert, who plays tennis so well, dance with George, chat in front of the fire with that dear intellectual Andrew (it will perhaps get you out of having to read Kafka for yourself), have your hair-drier repaired by that darling mechanically minded Peter, and keep your entire menagerie well in hand by feeding a simple diet of appropriate compliments.

Finally, if you are always on the look-out for opportunities to offer compliments, your entire point of view will change. You will see only the good side of people and you may even get to like them, which is perhaps one of the most foolproof recipes for happiness.

(See also Approval)

CONFESSION

How thrilling it is to share a deep, dark secret! All human beings even non-Catholics, feel the need one day or another to confess something that is weighing on their conscience. In fact psychoanalysts are not far from thinking that confession is the best cure for all mental illness. However, I will not attempt to discuss the merits of this therapy, only its application.

If you feel the need to reveal something in your past that obsesses you, choose as a confessor only a priest or a psychoanalyst, never someone you love. Even if the subject of your confession has nothing to do with him personally, there is no point in destroying the image he has of you. And if your bad deed does concern him, it is even less advisable to reveal it.

Nobody is obliged to confess past romantic experiences. When a man meets and marries a woman during the course of her voyage through life, it is only natural for him to accept her accompanying luggage. And you, madame, should feel the same toward your husband. His former mistresses are none of your business.

CONSCIENCE

A person's conscience is like a grandfather clock that constantly reminds us of every quarter of an hour that we have just wasted or spent unwisely.

CONTEMPT

Although hatred can be an indestructible bond between a couple, contempt is the death-knell of any relationship.

CONVALESCENCE

You can sigh with relief and know that your convalescent husband is getting better the day he starts to say disagreeable things to you; and he is definitely cured when he starts to shave again. If he has been very ill, he has become accustomed to being babied; he has even begun to enjoy staying in bed, having fresh sheets every day, receiving visits, being spoiled, being showered with sympathy and constant attention. Even the bliss of no longer suffering cannot make him forget that he is going to be deprived of all these extraordinary comforts, in short, that he will no longer be interesting; for, to himself, he is still as interesting as ever and you should never suggest that he isn't.

COOKING

Some men are very talented chefs and from time to time they condescend to prepare a complicated dish. Don't rejoice too quickly, for they have no intention of taking charge of an apple pie. No, the only thing they want is glory – as well as all the pots and pans in the house. With the money spent on the costly ingredients your chef-for-a-night will ask you to buy for him, you could feed the entire family for a week. So if you have a limited budget, make him do the shopping himself, telling him modestly that he is a much better shopper than you. Count on spending at least two hours cleaning the kitchen, the oven, the walls, the burned pots and pans, etc., and do not enter the sanctum sanctorum while he is officiating at the stove. When the famous dish is proudly brought into the dining-room, express the most delirious enthusiasm, lick your lips over it, but leave him the choicest morsels – which he will probably be eying greedily anyway. Afterwards, tell your friends about the fabulous meal he cooked for you. Nothing could please him more.

COQUETTE

A coquette may be an elegant woman who tried to make herself attractive, but she may also be a tease. You have undoubtedly met more than one woman who claims that she cannot pass a man in the street without his throwing himself at her and practically raping her. Although I like to think I was no less attractive than other girls when I was young, I cannot remember any such thing ever happening to me. The only women to whom explicit propositions are made are women who invite them. It's a game for them to collect admirers without the slightest intention of going any further. These are the women with the winking eyes, the moist lips and revealing sweaters who scream for help as soon as their attempts at seduction show signs of succeeding.

The next time you meet a tease, monsieur, if you wish either to teach her a lesson or to make her your eternally devoted slave, be the first to turn her down.

COUPLE

A marriage ceremony isn't always necessary in order to form a couple. In fact, many married people, unfortunately, form more of a vague partnership than a couple in the true sense of the word.

The combination of a short husband and a very tall wife always inspires smiles because, consciously or not, one always imagines a couple in bed. But the portrait of a perfect couple is moral as well as physical.

In order to form a true couple, each partner must draw his substance from the other, and I believe that you cannot really know a person, in business for example, as long as you haven't met his mate. A man who glowers whenever his secretary drops a pencil may be a tame and purring pet at home, obeying the orders of a petticoat tyrant. Another, a model of cordiality and courtesy during business hours, may be a veritable pocket dictator afterwards, with a terrorized wife who trembles before him.

Some couples, eternally in love, go through life hand in hand, and they should be shown on television throughout the entire world in order to inspire the others – the couples who haven't had anything to say to each other for ages. The former have never forgotten how to be attractive to each other. They have always laughed together at the same jokes, shared the same ambitions, practised the same sports and spent all their holidays together. They have lived in a closed circuit. Perhaps they have achieved this serenity only at the end of their lives, at the cost of sacrifices that have been repaid a hundredfold. But it was still necessary for them to be in love at the beginning, to admire each other, and to share the same tastes.

Some couples, too busy with careers and children

during the first thirty years of married life, make an effort to understand each other when they at last have time to do so, and they literally enjoy a first honeymoon at the end of their lives.

Others, whose marriage was merely a financial association at the beginning, exist only in public. They rush from one cocktail and dinner party to another, are perfect hosts and guests, tremble at the idea of spending an evening alone, and live on gossip and petits fours. They are couples only for show, and they can survive only in opulence.

But the majority of couples go on living together out of habit, cowardice, or fear of what-will-people-say. They are the most assiduous club members, their eyes shine and their wit sparkles only with strangers, and they distil around them an inexpressible boredom that is as perceptible as the scent of moth-balls diffused in October by a garment that has been packed away all summer long.

Finally, some couples – many more than you may think – are united by a virulent hatred which they cannot do without and which at least helps them to live intensely. This is the case of the couple in *Virginia Woolf*, and who wouldn't be afraid of her?

If I knew the exact, infallible formula for creating one of the first two kinds of couples I have described, and for avoiding turning into one of the others, I suppose that this book would soon be a best-seller. But alas, such a formula doesn't exist. However, if you try throughout your life to think more of your mate than of yourself, if you respect his tastes, thoughts and ambitions, if, instead of destroying him day by day as water erodes mountains, you bring him one stone after another with which to fortify his own personality, if you bind up his wounds, if you are his music, his champagne and his sunshine – then there is a very good chance that you will succeed in forming a true couple.

COURAGE

There are so many different kinds of courage that it is very often hard to know what is courageous and what is not. But in general the word 'courage' is associated with exceptionally dazzling deeds more often than with daily actions that nevertheless require a great deal of perseverance.

Courage is an essential ingredient of the perfect man with a capital M! He is expected to plunge into the Thames to save somebody from drowning, or to floor an assailant with a well-aimed right to the chin. Spectacular acts of courage require above all strong muscles and rapid reflexes which fill ordinary people with admiration, although very few of them consider how much persistent courage it takes to become a great pianist, an erudite professor or a doctor – not to mention the courage, even more heroic because it is completely unrewarded, a man must have in order to get up early every morning and go off to a tiresome job that scarcely pays enough to keep him alive.

A woman's role is to help the men in her life discover in themselves a courage they perhaps never knew they had, and you can be sure that in the shadow of every courageous man there has been a mother, a sister, a wife or a daughter who encouraged him at one time or another.

COURTSHIP

We are far removed from troubadors, 'tenderness cards', and even from the established rites our grandfathers used to practise when they courted our grandmothers.

Modern men certainly haven't the same methods as their predecessors, and the result is approximately as follows:

At 16: Would you like to dance?

At 18: Would you like to study Schopenhauer with me?

At 20: Are you going to So-and-So's party?

At 22: How about going on to Arthur's?

At 25: How about a weekend in the country?

At 30: How about a weekend in the country?

At 35: How about a weekend in the country?

At 40: How about a weekend in the country?

At 50: How about a weekend in Paris?

At 70: I have a good income and a nice house in le Touquet . . .

At any rate, it proves that men become more and more sensitive to cold as they grow older!

CREDIT

I know that the entire British economy is based on credit. Young people want to own everything right away, undoubtedly with the idea at the back of their minds that the sky may fall on their heads tomorrow, so they must hurry up and enjoy life today.

Then there is ruthless advertising, reminding everyone by sight and sound that men are men only if they own a certain make of car, use a certain brand of aftershave, or brush their teeth with a certain kind of toothpaste; that a woman is worth looking at only if she washes her dishes or her hair with certain products; that a child can develop well only if he possesses a certain toy, and that even a puppy can aspire to a happy dog's life only if he laps up a certain dog food!

The hero of modern times is the man who possesses sufficient strength of character to resist all these temptations, and my French mind is not far from comparing contemporary credit facilities to the temptations of St Anthony: they are purely and simply a manifestation of the Devil. I have queried a lot of worried-looking young husbands, and all of them admitted that if they could do it all over again they would refrain from incurring debts at the start of their married lives.

And so, young bride, if you wish your marriage to be a great success and if you don't want to lay the groundwork for a heart attack for your husband during the very first days of wedded life, instead of insisting on having every comfort right away as well as all the more or less practical gadgets that are proposed to you twenty-four hours a day in the newspapers and on television, take a careful look at your overall budget and say to yourself that if you buy one thing more you will have to cut down somewhere else. Besides, you never feel as if you really own an object until it has been completely paid for, and I know of nothing more demoralizing than to go on paying for something that is already worn out. You must realize that all these amiable people who are so anxious to offer you credit are far from being smiling philanthropists. They earn their living from it – from that extra money you pay them because you haven't wanted to wait.

Do you know why companies prefer to engage married men rather than bachelors? Simply because they know that a married man is assailed with such demands for money that he works much harder in order to pay his debts. Could anything be more cynical!

CRITICISM

I am sure that more divorces have been caused by a climate of mutual criticism than by the infidelity of one of the two partners.

Even when criticism is offered in good faith with the intention of rendering a service, it should always be expressed with a maximum of tact and it should always be counterbalanced by a compliment. For example, it is much easier to accept a criticism along the lines of: 'Don't you think that high neckline hides your lovely neck?' 'Or I wonder if the colour of that sofa doesn't detract from the marvellous colour scheme you've arranged in the living-room' – rather than: 'You shouldn't wear high necklines, they make you look hunchbacked', or 'That sofa ruins the entire living-room'. The only criticism that isn't completely negative is the one that is offered in order to prevent someone from making a mistake in a purchase or a decision; in other circumstances, criticism only serves to make you unpopular.

As for couples who spend their lives criticizing each other in public, you should eliminate their names from your address-book. It must be admitted that husbands and wives generally refrain from criticizing each other in public, but this doesn't make the criticism they get at home any more pleasant. And so, monsieur, after a dinner your wife took a lot of trouble over, don't point out that the roast was overdone – besides, she noticed it long before you did. As for you, madame, you are not always very tactful or very fair when it comes to criticizing your husband. Instead of praising the elegance of Paul's suits or Peter's neckties, buy your husband what he needs; and instead of telling him that he doesn't know how to get ahead in business as well as Jack, try to help him find a way to improve your end-of-the-month figures. The goal of marriage is not to test one's mate, awarding a mark in every subject, but rather to join forces in solving all life's problems.

Critical wit is amusing only when it is used to ridicule others, and while masters of mockery always find an attentive audience in social life, they seldom inspire either true love or devoted friendship. A genuine sense of humour is not concerned with tearing other people apart, but with refusing to take oneself seriously. So before marrying a caustic wit who has nothing nice to say about anybody, you should realize that you will soon become the favourite target of his sarcasm, and that life with him is more apt to be a painful ordeal than a perpetual peal of laughter.

(See also Advice, Reproaches)

CULTURE

If you meet a man who is as elegant as the Duke of Westminster, as brilliant in business as Aristotle Onassis, but who has never had any time to develop his mind whereas you are the intellectual type – never, never fall in love with him. You will only die of boredom on his yacht.

Culture procures joys and pleasures that all the money in the world cannot buy. On the other hand, an extremely cultured man may enjoy playing the role of Pygmalion, expending treasures of patience to improve the mind of the woman he loves.

In society you meet more people who have acquired a thin veneer of culture than people who are genuinely cultured, and it is never advisable to probe too deeply into the learning of social acquaintances if you wish to remain popular. If you are an expert in Sumerian art, don't attempt to dazzle everybody with your erudition, for they will only yawn. Men listen appreciatively only to people who have been paid to lecture to them, and in this case the speaker is never brilliant enough for their taste.

DANCING

Dancing is either an erotic or a primitive religious phenomenon, the effect of which is comparable with that of drugs. The less civilized a society, the better its members dance to express their joy, since rhythm is a very difficult thing to acquire if you haven't been born with it. Ballroom dancing, with two partners enlaced, lasted no more than the space of a century – the very same century that was noted for its individualism and revolutionary ideas. Today people dance alone, which may augur the total independence of women who, even on the dance floor, no longer want to be led. Dancing in groups of ten instead of two by two is merely one more proof of the domination of the individual by the collective, as well as a form of release from it and an attempt at communication which has become increasingly rare and ephemeral.

But to descend from our lofty philosophical heights, here is some advice for young girls:

It used to be very important for a girl to be a good

dancer and the best dancers were the most popular girls at a ball. Now, however, since a girl can perfectly well invite a boy to a dance, she is no longer haunted by the fear of being a wallflower. Even so, boys don't like to be pursued and if they don't seem enthusiastic about dancing with you, don't persist or they will soon give you the reputation of being a gluepot. Beware also of over-suggestive movements which might seem to promise what you are not yet prepared to accord. On the other hand, too much stiffness would reveal your complexes and perhaps frighten away a boy who might have become interested in you. Beyond a certain age it is better to watch than to participate in these savage rites which are too much for older adults. If you still love to dance all night, take a cruise on a ship – the captain is always an expert in the one-step!

DATES

You have a date for Saturday night. You've thought of everything: your dress, new stockings, hairdresser, perfume – but have you thought of your conversation? It will be the first time he has taken you out and he is probably as scared as you are. You must therefore put him at ease at once, and it might not be such a bad idea to refrain from wearing your most elegant ensemble. Rather, try to be as natural as possible and don't over-whelm him with a stereotyped smile or with a sophisticated voice like the receptionist in a snobbish beauty salon. Simply tell him how glad you are to see him, what a good mood you're in, how marvellous the weather is, and respond with enthusiasm to all his suggestions for the evening's entertainment. After this kind of treatment, you will probably be booked up for the next fifty-one Saturday nights of the year – and you will have plenty of time to get him to do what you really enjoy.

(See also Blind Dates)

DELICACIES

Prepare a gastronomic little dinner from time to time, without waiting for holidays and birthdays. Imagination and surprises – that's what a marriage needs to keep from gradually sinking into the quicksands of boredom.

But if he has told you that he adores chocolate mousse, don't serve it to him once a week. He will suffer in silence for a year or two until he finally explodes and confesses that he cannot swallow another spoonful of it.

(See also Appetite)

DESIRE

Some men think they are paying us the most supremely flattering compliment when they tell us that they 'want' us. The approach is a little primitive, because a woman who has never excited the desire of any man must really be completely repulsive, judging from the number of unattractive pregnant women you see in the streets.

We never explain emphatically enough to young girls that the desire men feel for them does not take the same form as the desire they may feel toward a man, and they shouldn't weep if he snores very soon afterwards while they are still as vibrant as a harp in the wind, nor should they blame themselves if their partner simply isn't in the mood one night. Masculine desire is an extremely delicate mechanism that women do not always understand very well, even after thirty years of marriage.

DIAMONDS

Men who offer diamonds are either very rich or very much in love. Conclusion: Hurrah for diamonds!

DIARY

You are your husband's social secretary. You should remind him in advance of all the dinner parties and other social engagements you've arranged by entering them in his diary. You might also make a note of your birthday – it can avoid tearful scenes.

As for your own diary, if you are leading a double life I suppose it is too exciting for there to be any risk of forgetting your rendezvous. In any case, it is certainly inadvisable to put them down in writing.

DIETS

Your husband returns from a visit to his doctor with a diet banning everything he likes to eat. He's in a black mood. Life doesn't seem worth living with no salt, no whisky and no desserts.

Instead of saying that it won't be much fun for you either to have to plan menus composed of grilled lean meat, tell him that you know a thousand different recipes, that it hasn't the slightest importance, and that it would do you a lot of good to follow the same diet. Then avoid all possible temptations even when there are guests for dinner. Vary your menus as much as possible, present them in an appetizing manner, and never forget to compliment him on how well he looks, thanks to all his sacrifices: he seems so much younger, his clothes hang better, he's never short of breath any more, etc.

But if it is you who have been given a diet, or if you simply decide to reduce, you should plan two separate menus. Never serve him a green salad and nothing else.

DINNER

Dinner-time should always be a moment of relaxation after a tiring day, and an event that the entire family awaits with impatience.

A successful dinner consists of two ingredients: the menu and the conversation, both of which should be varied. You should therefore develop your cooking talents and avoid repeating the same dish every Thursday, but try out new and original recipes. Even if some of them may not merit compliments, they will at least provide a subject of conversation.

If there are many of you seated around the dinner-table, try to make each person shine in turn; and if you are lucky enough to have a talkative husband, let him speak without interruption.

A happy marriage is simply a series of successful dinners.

(See also Appetite)

DISPOSITION

A glowering eye, a frowning brow, a slamming door, – he's in a bad mood. Well, this isn't the day to ask him for anything, and especially not to ask him why he's in such a foul temper, because it goes without saying that you pretend not to notice it. You smile, you pay no attention to his silence and leave the room. If there is nobody present on whom to vent his bad temper, it will die out like a fire that is deprived of oxygen.

It may be amusing to play the part of a petty tyrant and to create a tempest in a teapot, but if the role ever tempts you, remember that nothing is more tiresome for the people around you. A man or woman who suffers from a chronic case of bad disposition runs the risk of facing a lonely old age.

(See also Temperament)

DISTRESS

When a woman whose car has broken down raises the bonnet and contemplates the suddenly silent motor with an air of bewilderment, it has the same effect as if she had hoisted a distress signal. And women should make the most of it while they can, for in a few years it will probably be they who will have to come to the aid of men, or perhaps nobody will help anybody in distress any more.

And yet it used to be pleasant and practical to turn to men for aid and protection. The privilege of changing our tyres ourselves seems to me a dubious victory prize. Let's hope that there will still remain some lazy, old-fashioned women, like myself, who will retard progress and the battle for equality, and that all big-hearted, well-muscled men will not relinquish their places behind the steering-wheel to their sisters.

But you shouldn't overdo an act of helplessness in which nobody believes any more. Women must choose once and for all between wearing the trousers and doing the hard work, or being lazy and obedient.

DIVORCE

'To err is human' – and the idea of indissoluble marriage is rather intimating.

But there is no point in getting married if you don't believe that it will be forever. Accidents may occur along the way, but at least you ought to start out with the idea of reaching the end of the road together. A divorce is like a recipe that didn't turn out: it always leaves a rather bad taste in your mouth.

It is obvious that if a woman has had the bad luck to marry a man who drinks, gambles, is dishonest or brutal, she is perfectly right to seek a divorce as quickly as possible in order to have the best chance of remaking a happier life.

Since every unsuccessful marriage is a special case, it is difficult to lay down general rules and principles, so I shall confine myself to an analysis of a few common examples:

– Newly wed, you notice that your husband is already being unfaithful to you. You will probably never succeed in curing him of his vagabond nature, and it is preferable to realize that you have made a mistake as soon as possible, before he has had time to provide you with a swarm of children.

– Ten or twenty years have passed – years of cloudless happiness made up of joys and pains shared day by day, and then crash! One fine day, nothing in the world exists for him except some tall, raven-haired beauty or some mousy little blonde. He is ready to abandon everything for her and he begs you for a divorce. Is it better to be patient or to give him his freedom in a gesture of magnanimity? I must confess that personally I would probably not behave very elegantly and would hang on to him in the hope of an eventual change of heart. But my daughter tells me that I am old-fashioned and that unless a woman is completely mad about a man she must have the soul of a martyr or else be slightly masochistic in order to submit to infidelity and ridicule, and that resistance will only inspire the hatred and scorn of a man who was, until then, very fond of you.

It seems to me that you can always separate for a certain period of time. But avoid a definite rupture in the hope that your husband's great love will vanish as suddenly as it appeared, and that you are really doing him a service by preventing him from marrying a woman for whom his apparent passion may be merely a passing fancy.

But if, at the end of these same ten or twenty years, you no longer have anything in common, if you live together like two more or less courteous strangers, if even your children seem to divide rather than to strengthen your union, it is certainly more honest to ratify this moral separation by getting a legal divorce. How many couples are there who no longer have anything in common apart from their last name, who do not even live together, and whom no hostess would even dream of inviting to the same party?

It is very common to see couples remain together until their children are married, or to separate as soon as they have discharged the obligations of the children's education. This behaviour is certainly preferable when the couple in question is sufficiently self-controlled to refrain from quarrelling all day long. But if the children will have to live in an explosive atmosphere, it is much better to provide them with two separate but peaceful homes. In this case, the principal danger for the child is that he will be twice as spoiled – spoiled in the literal sense of the word – because there may be four people vying for his love instead of two, and none of the four wishes to assume the responsibility of punishing him or of giving him a real education. I shall never forget the ecstatic reaction of my eleven-year-old daughter to the escalation of treats which the divorced parents of her boarding-school chum felt obliged to employ in order to win the child's affection. She wrote to us: 'What a pity you aren't divorced. Muriel gets twice as many gift parcels as I do!'

Between the two extremes of ostracism, which was our grandmothers' attitude towards divorcees, and the modern tendency of divorced people to invite their ex-husbands or ex-wives to their latest wedding, there is undoubtedly a middle road, to which good taste alone can guide us. Furthermore, you really must be completely lacking in imagination if you can bear the sight of a man whose anatomy and mannerisms are familiar to you in their slightest details, when he has become the husband of somebody else, even if your feelings toward him have cooled to the point of indifference. But will you ever be able to feel mere indifference toward him? It seems to me impossible. Either he is the innocent victim – and it is never pleasant to be brought face to face with one's bad deeds; or you yourself are the victim and you feel regret or bitterness at the sight of him; and if both of you are equally guilty, it is not agreeable to be confronted with one's past mistakes either.

But as people divorce more and more easily all over the world and for the most absurd reasons, I suppose that one day there will be no point in going to all the bother of getting married in the first place.

If you marry a divorced man, you should realize that you are running certain risks, especially if he has been divorced several times, for this is proof that he either lacks judgment or is impossible to live with. Even if he is comfortably wealthy, you will surely be irritated by the sight of the cheques he will have to send each month to his former wife or wives. Finally, the role of step-mother is rather unflattering and even slightly ridiculous when the children are your own age.

If you are a divorcée, rich and getting on in years, try to resist the temptation of treating yourself to a beau who is very much younger than you are. May and December romances, which are quite common with sixty-year-old millionaires who end up by marrying twenty-year-old girls, are also becoming more frequent among women who enjoy the income from several alimony settlements. The spectre of old age has always been frightening, but at least age used to be respected, whereas nowadays it is often turned to ridicule. And so we see women of sixty or more, with their lifted faces, their surgically reinforced bosoms, their silky wigs and false eyelashes, becoming infatuated with charming young men who are thirty years junior to them. Gigolos have always existed in certain circles, but it seems that they are now taking the place of the chorus girl of our father's time, as more and more money passes into the hands of women.

This is not to say that youthful company should be avoided. On the contrary, it is far more stimulating than that of old people. But an older woman must be completely devoid of decency or self-respect in order to dare offer her decadent body to a very young man, even if he puts on a fairly convincing act of romantic love. Women who think they are thus postponing the inevitable age of retirement should be prepared for a rude awakening the day when, having exhausted every artificial aid, they find themselves all alone with their wrinkles, their disillusionment and the scorn of their own generation.

(See also Alimony, Ex-husbands)

DO-IT-YOURSELF

Well-performed manual labour not only gives great satisfaction but is also very practical. In our age when artisans have practically disappeared, there are many advantages in marrying a handy man rather than golfer. But if your handy man's greatest pleasure comes from possessing the complete equipment of a perfect cabinet-maker, television repairman or plumber, you should be warned that the cost of these fancy tools may very well amount to even more than the cost of hiring a specialist – without forgetting that you'll sometimes wonder where in the world you will find the room to store them all!

DON JUANS

Don Juans can be placed in the same category as drug addicts and alcoholics. They are all sick men who try by some means or other to forget their own personalities, which they dislike.

However, they are still surrounded by a certain aura of virility, and while we pity and give medical treatment to drug addicts and alcoholics, it has never occurred to anybody to give a disintoxication treatment to Don Juans, even though they have the greatest need for it. The widespread personal publicity promulgated by Don Juans in order to reassure themselves and to prove to themselves that they are wonderful – which they certainly don't believe deep down in their hearts – should be sufficient warning for a woman. While an innocent young girl may be forgiven for believing in the romantic speeches, the passionate panting and the smouldering glances of a Don Juan in sheep's clothing, it is inexcusable and degrading for an experienced woman to be taken in by a professional.

Mr Don Juan likes women the way a hunter likes pheasant: he simply wants to bag the greatest possible number of them. The only thing that amuses him is the chase or the accurately aimed shot. Women and game lose all interest as soon as the first is in bed and the second has been downed.

Should a woman decide to let herself succumb to a Don Juan, if only out of curiosity, she is almost certain to be disappointed, because the vice of this type of man is to be too much in love with himself and not to give the slightest thought to his partner's pleasure.

Moreover, in this day and age a vice is simply a form of malady . . . and maladies can be treated.

DREAMS

Recent research on dreams has shown that everybody dreams and that if we are deprived of dreams we die – cats in four days and men a little later.

But as in the case of everything else in life, while we may need to dream a little, it would be dangerous to do nothing else. A man who is a little dreamer may be more charming than a man who goes through life with a stop-watch in one hand and a calendar in the other, but the end of the month is apt to be much more agonizing.

Nowadays daydreaming is a luxury few women can afford. Nevertheless, there are a few moments during the day when it is very refreshing to dream. My bathtub, for example, is the theatre of fabulous exploits of which I am, needless to say, the heroine, and which fill my entire day with optimism; all the disagreeable little incidents seem to slide off the laurels I've gathered while soaking in my tub.

DRINKERS

Frankly, I have no greater liking for men who don't drink at all than for those who drink too much.

Bragging that you never touch a glass of wine or a drop of liquor amounts to confessing that you have either a weak stomach or a narrow mind and, since you apparently haven't the strength to stop in time, that you have no will-power. The ascetic or Puritan who deprives himself of all the pleasures of life often betrays a certain emotional avarice, and it is significant that people who thank heaven for all the good things found on earth are called 'bon vivants' or 'good livers'.

The essential rule of life of a civilized man is moderation. Confident that he will not let himself indulge to excess, he can enjoy all life's pleasures. He is a gourmet but not a gourmand, a lover but not a Don Juan, refined but not a fuss-budget, a connoisseur but not a collector. The man who drinks too much does so for various reasons, which finally can be summarized in a single one: he is dissatisfied with himself.

Liquor is a stimulant which he cannot do without as soon as the conversation around him no longer concerns him any more than the hum of city traffic, and as soon as he feels dead inside. A drink then provides him with a synthetic interest in life and it loosens his tongue –

before paralysing it definitively. Finally, the drinker feels happy with himself and even admires himself for being so lucid. If the effects of alcohol could stop at this point and if drinkers were content to be supermen only on Saturday nights, there would be no alcoholics. Unfortunately, the more a man drinks the thirstier he becomes, and he ends up unable to face life except from behind the protective screen of alcohol.

If you notice that your husband requires a stimulant every day, don't dismiss the fact as unimportant, but try to distract him by every possible means. Get him to drink wine with his meals instead of two martinis beforehand. Certain pastimes such as cards encourage drinking; others, such as sports, prevent it. You can ask your doctor to give him a scare, but first of all start by asking yourself if you are as solicitous, as flirtatious, as attractive as you were when he first met you. If you are honest with yourself, I should be surprised if you haven't changed a little bit, because the majority of men who drink excessively are simply husbands who are bored.

DRIVERS

In spite of the statistics proving that women have less accidents than men do, men never fail to snigger whenever some poor woman has trouble manoeuvring her car into a tight parking-space. They are so delighted when it is a woman driver who causes a traffic jam that they almost forget they are going to be late. A sort of masculine solidarity builds up from car to car and they use all the most colourful terms they can invent in order to make fun of that 'crazy woman driver'.

Even the worst kind of Don Juan, who generally throws himself at any skirt in sight, forgets the elementary rules of his profession of seduction and joins the male chorus of intrepid and irreproachable drivers.

When one of these men has an accident, he never admits that it might have been his fault. But if his unfortunate wife puts a little dent in a bumper, how enthusiastically he assails her with sarcastic remarks!

A man must be really very tired in order to let his wife do the driving. Men cannot tolerate a woman's showing the slightest sign of fear when they are at the wheel, but when the positions are reversed they make no effort to conceal their terror, even if there isn't the slightest danger in sight.

I have never met a man who was willing to admit that his wife was a better driver than he, even if the evidence was flagrant. It is perhaps in this instance that men show their most glaring bad faith.

(See also Cars)

EGOTISM

It is the most comfortable attitude in the world to think only of oneself. The universe will necessarily be somewhat shrunken, but that doesn't matter because an inflated ego can fill the entire horizon. While an egotist loves only himself, he still doesn't mind being loved, and he accords a certain degree of interest to others only when they return his affection a hundredfold.

Everybody admits that men are generally much more egotistical than women by their very nature — which is to receive what women give them. This state of affairs will doubtless never change, and the best thing to do is to accept it philosophically. However, since it would be better not to marry an egocentric, here are a few signs that will betray his true character before it is too late:

— In restaurants, he suggests a menu without waiting for you to make your own choice.

— He adores chocolates while you prefer caramels; but the boxes of sweets he brings you always contain chocolates.

– He gives you the latest hot novel for your birthday, adding casually that he would love to read it when you have finished with it.

– When you go to the films together, it is always he who chooses the film.

– If, in addition, he adores canoeing and poker, beware! Before you know it you will spend all your holidays shooting the most violently churning rapids, and every Sunday his poker-playing friends will transform your living-room into a gambling den and you into a barmaid.

ELECTRICITY

In Europe, electric plugs and sockets are referred to as 'male' and 'female', and when I was young I always blushed whenever I heard the terms. Today, I consider it a marvellous symbolism, for it is perfectly true that enlightenment, or even an effect of dazzlement, can occur only when both of them are perfectly adapted to each other.

ELEGANCE

Although a man has less chance of making a mistake in his manner of dress than does a woman, it is also more difficult for him to achieve elegance; in fact there are very few really elegant men.

Here is the recipe for a cocktail that is rather difficult to mix well – that of an elegant man:

In a mould that is at least 5ft. 6in. and not more than 6ft. 6in. high, weighing between 130 and 190 pounds:

Mix together:
 a few muscles, but not bulging ones
 a beautiful deep voice
 the serene assurance of 'the right man in the right
  place'
 nice hair – or no hair
 but a well-shaven face, with or without a
  moustache
 and a little hair elsewhere.

Add:
 a twist of humour
 2 drops of the milk of human kindness to make his
  eyes shine.

Heat to the proper temperature – which is between that of a Swedish iceberg and a Sicilian volcano.
And garnish with clothing that is so suitable as to be hardly noticeable.

This recipe can just as well produce a British Prime Minister as a Neapolitan fisherman, a white-coated surgeon or a Texas cowboy. So I shall say once more that elegance has only the vaguest relationship to money or fashion, and that it is made up of intelligence, suitability to a certain society and set of circumstances, the joy of living and, incidentally, plenty of soap.

ELOPEMENT

This romantic tradition has completely gone out of fashion. Ladders set up in the middle of the night against bedroom balconies disappeared together with parental authority.

ENOUGH

A sense of moderation, tact, a recognition of one's limitations, of one's age, and even of the capacity of one's stomach, are all notions that help us to get along well in an organized society.

Good manners consist of knowing when to say: 'That's enough!'

– Knowing how to leave when your hosts yawn.

– Knowing how to refuse the third whisky.

– Knowing at what age a woman can no longer dress the way her daughter does.

– Knowing how to say 'no' to the man who wants to see you home . . . and to tuck you up in bed.

– Knowing how to remain silent when the conversation is beyond your depth.

ENTERTAINING

'Entertaining' means receiving guests and also amusing them, and that is exactly what I suggest that you do for all the men in your family. From grandfather to grandson, every man is happy to come home when he knows he is being awaited with pleasure and impatience. As for your husband, put on your lipstick before he comes home. Then, instead of weighing him down with a recital of all your woes, try to have something amusing to tell him – a bit of gossip, for instance (men enjoy gossip much more than they are willing to admit), or simply a newspaper article.

If you don't want your son to consider your home as a combination restaurant, dormitory and free laundry, you must treat him, too, like a guest and refrain from wasting the little time you have together in scolding him for his poor marks at school or criticizing the way he wears his hair. Without going so far as to organize a game of musical chairs for the entire household, it is nevertheless up to you to invent the rites and family fun that turn a house into a home.

EROTICISM

Once the source of forbidden pleasures, today eroticism has become the avowed goal of numerous activities and the unavowed theme of almost all advertising. Everyone believes he has a right to his little quarter of an hour of eroticism every day, and people who dare confess their ignorance of the subject are immediately sent to the nearest psychiatrist.

I don't mean to imply that we should minimize the force and attraction of sensual pleasure, but it is confusing heaven and earth to equate eroticism and love. One is no more than the recompense of the other, and while love almost always engenders pleasure, the contrary is seldom true. Furthermore, at the extreme limit, nymphomania, alcoholism and drugs are three absolutely similar vices, all equally degrading, since all of them seek release in the same intoxication from personal dissatisfaction or absolute solitude.

So, viewed in its most absurd form, eroticism as an end in itself betrays an imprisoning egocentricity – and is therefore the exact opposite of love.

EX-HUSBANDS

You were sufficiently in love to think that you could spend the rest of your lives together, and then crash! You can no longer stand the sight of one another and the man who you believed was *the* man in your life becomes your 'Ex'. All of a sudden a person whose slightest idiosyncrasies and most hidden beauty-spots were no secrets to you becomes a stranger whom you try to avoid encountering. My mother never saw my father once during the thirty years between the day they were divorced and the day she died; she used to send me to have lunch with him every other Thursday and to spend two weeks in September with my grandparents. They refrained from speaking ill of each other, but they also refrained from asking after each other; both of them had rebuilt their lives, retaining fond memories of their youth, but developing a mutual feeling of indifference. Perhaps this is the best kind of relationship with an ex-husband when there still remain financial problems to be settled, and especially when children are involved. In this regard, while I find it abnormal for a man to pay exorbitant sums of money to an ex-wife who is young and able to work, simply because he was married to her for a brief moment, it is perfectly normal for him to pay for the education and care of his children, even long after they are of age, or for him to be obliged to support in the manner to which she is accustomed an ageing wife he has discarded in order to marry a younger woman.

Modern psychologists insist on the importance of paternal authority in bringing up children; it is therefore necessary to arrange things so that the children don't feel deprived of a father, and you should never try to cut down on the visiting times allotted to him. Finally, even if a couple has been separated for years and each one has remarried, they should join together again on their child's wedding day. It seems to me that if I were married to a man who already had children from a previous marriage, I would arrange to make an urgent visit to a sick old aunt in Manchester in order to avoid imposing my presence on the original family circle that should be formed again for just one day. In short, a woman's relations with her ex-husband should be primarily dignified and devoid of emotion – to all appearances, at least. (See also Alimony, Divorce)

EXPENSES

Men and women haven't at all the same point of view where spending money is concerned:

– Men light-heartedly spend a great deal of money for a pleasant evening; restaurants, night clubs and, in Japan, geishas, who cost a fortune.

– Women consider entertaining at home.

– Men spend in splurges. They buy new clothes for the entire family some Saturday morning, or practically clean out a grocers shop for no particular reason.

– Women know that they have only so much money per week to spend on household expenses and food.

– Men succumb to the temptation of all sorts of utterly useless gadgets.

– Women dream of labour-saving devices.

– Men buy what they see on display, and they like clearly marked price tags.

– Women go into a shop 'to look around' and to find a bargain.

– Men buy their wives jewellery in order to enhance their own prestige.

– Women buy jewellery in order to be more beautiful.

– Men buy motors.

– Women buy chassis.

– Men spend the most on their hobbies.

– Women spend the most on their appearance.

. . . and the art of creating a happy marriage is perhaps

for each one to accept the other's expenses with a smile. (See also Budget)

EXPENSIVE

A woman who gives the impression of being extremely rich will attract gigolos and discourage honest men. The latter will think they can never offer her anything more than she already has, and they will reluctantly give her up like an article that is too expensive for them.

The tragic destiny of very rich women is always to give, without ever being able to receive.

EYES

The only true international idiom is the language of the eyes, and yet it is not exactly the same in all countries. An Italian who makes eyes at you is simply being polite, but I would be quite astonished if a Japanese did the same.

Without going so far as the women found in every port who employ a special kind of mimicry in order to attract sailors on leave there are certain more civilized glances that are filled with meaning.

For example, the gentlemen who obviously has eyes only for your lips and bosom as you talk, and you say to yourself: 'I see what he's after . . . there's no point in my trying to be witty'; the woman who looks you up and down with an unfriendly air and squinting eyes when you enter a restaurant: 'Good! I must look attractive tonight!'; the man who is constantly looking past you as you're talking to him: 'I've missed the boat, he's not the least bit interested in me'; the woman who flutters her eyelashes or opens her eyes wide, the way a police car flashes its revolving spotlight: 'As for you, my pet, you must be interested in my husband!'

Then there is the disappointed suitor who gazes deep into your eyes for minutes that seem like hours; and the shy man whose glance you never succeed in catching; and the good friend whose look is frank and untroubled . . . What a lot of things can be said with the eyes!

FAIRY TALES

Cinderella's slipper has been replaced by the X brassière . . . and the Sleeping Beauty is awakened by the scent of Prince Charming's after-shave lotion or simply by the aroma of Z instant coffee. But deep down in our hearts we still believe in fairy tales. Otherwise, how can you explain the fantastic commercial success of beauty creams and even of household products? Life would be unbearable without miracles and without Prince Charmings. So let's be thankful to advertising for wielding the last remaining magic wand. Every era has the fairies it deserves.

FAMILY SPIRIT

Chauvinism, clan and family spirit can make life difficult for foreigners in a country or outsiders to a religion, a political party, a school or simply a family unit. Certain families do not readily assimilate new members, and they expect from a new bride or groom total submission together with a rejection of the outsider's own family and inherited traditions.

If you have married into such a domineering family, there are two possibilities: either your husband is dependent on them and you have no choice but to bend to their customs and ways in order to be accepted as quickly as possible; or else he is completely independent, and you would do well to sever the umbilical cord that still attaches him to his mother by moving to some other part of the country while he is still madly in love with you – because afterwards it will be too late.

Traditions are certainly of value, but families – like conquering nations – can make themselves detested by trying to impose them on others, even though they may be convinced that their way of life is the most civilized in the world.

FATHERS

Three hundred years at the most separate the patriarch possessing the power of life or death over his family from the Virgin Birth, and there is only a century between the child martyr of Dickens, who turned his meagre earnings over to his parents from the age of six, and the child-king of today, to whom all is due. What has happened to the modern father to have made him end up 'in the closet', according to the famous play?[1]

It cannot even be claimed that he has relinquished

---

[1] Oh Dad, Poor Dad, Mama's Hung You in the Closet and I'm Feelin' So Sad!

his powers to his wife, who has acquired more rights on paper than in reality; his authority has simply disappeared and it has not been replaced. This can perhaps be explained by the fact that the family home has lost its character of an inviolable haven and become merely a place of rest where peace and quiet are sought above all else, or by the fact that the government increasingly provides for everything – illness, old age, Social Security, etc. In any case, the fact is there: modern man has failed even more as a father than he has as a husband, and there is no need to look any further for the principal causes of juvenile delinquency.

There are three types of father:

1. The Paterfamilias, master after God, an antique species fast becoming obsolete. He is also a tyrannical husband, his word is never questioned – not because he is always right but because he shouts the loudest. Throughout the years he takes away desserts, locks in bedrooms, cuts off allowances and banishes from home the daughter-who-has-sinned. He generally succeeds merely in creating a stronger attachment between the mother and her children, in being hoodwinked and cheated, but at least, until he finds himself completely abandoned by everybody, he is feared – and that is all he wants. If you have a husband of this type, it is probable that he is not extremely tender with you either, and that he insists on checking up on everything. The best thing to do is to get a job, if only in order to enjoy a little income so as to palliate his avarice and permit you to

offer treats to your children on the sly. Patiently wait for him to calm down or to feel the need for a little affection himself one day. It is more than probable that his grandchildren will twist him around their little fingers. As a matter of fact, it is much wiser to let your daughter deal with him and even to teach her how to handle him. While showing him the greatest respect and even a little fear, train her to climb up on his knees, to tell him how handsome he is, and that she will only marry a man like him: he is a proud male, even more sensitive than other types of men. She can even plead your cause for you and especially that of her brother, because these men seldom get along with their sons, who never seem to be equal to the ambitions their fathers cherish for them. I have seen these terrors literally twisted around the little finger of a coy and clever little girl.

2. The Father-Pal. Having become a father at too early an age, he has never had time to grow up. Besides, he doesn't want to grow old at any price. And so, instead of raising his children in the true sense of the word, he lowers himself to their level and believes that, by being their pal and by competing with them in all their sports, he will win their love and confidence. He wants to know all about his son's love life and believes it is sufficient for him to use the same language, to slap him on the back and to let himself be called 'Paul' rather than 'Dad' in order to pull it off. All the young people I know loathe being exploited in this way, and when I asked them to describe their ideal father, they were unanimous in

saying that what they most dislike is overfamiliarity and that a father should always keep some distance. They sense perfectly well that what they need is a guide and not a pal. If you have a husband who doesn't know how to make himself respected, try to get him to understand that an over-age Boy Scout is always ridiculous, and that it is a mistake for him to lose his breath in pursuit of his lost youth. Explain to him tactfully that his children may prefer to seek advice from more serious adults who inspire greater confidence, and above all greater respect. Finally, try to make him seem more important at home. As a matter of fact, it is very rare for the family of a man who occupies a responsible position to have an opportunity to see him in the full exercise of his authority, and this is a pity because the primary duty of a father is to make himself admired by his family.

3. The Drop-out Father. The most common type of father in all the highly civilized countries, he has undoubtedly sired his children without paying very much attention and he considers that by working hard in order to house them, feed them, clothe them, educate them and send them to the seaside in summer he is amply fulfilling his duty. When he comes home at night he desires peace above all, and family problems tire him. If, gradually discouraged by his failure to play his role as head of the family, you have replaced him, he will retire more and more into his tent and behind his newspaper and he will soon be no more useful around the house than a robot that dispenses money. Soon your

children will come home only when they need to ask for money and to have their laundry done. Don't cry over it – because it is your own fault. The authority of a husband and father is like a plant; it needs to be cared for. And it is you who, not satisfied to see it droop, have knowingly let it dry out every day to the profit of your own. You began by signing poor report cards and ended up by fibbing about how late the children came home from a night out or by paying the fines or repair bills on the car they 'borrowed'. So the day a major catastrophe arrives, don't be astonished if you have to handle it alone and, feminine logic being what it is, don't attack your husband with unjustified reproaches. Ever since the day your children were born, you should have let him look after them too. I see nothing at all ridiculous in a young father's knowing how to change a baby's nappies or give a bottle. Later on, even when he comes home tired from work, insist that he help the children with their homework and, on Sunday, plan an outing for them together. In short, try to help them get to know each other.

From time to time these last two categories of fathers are seized by a brief fever of tyranny like the first. They suddenly realize that the family is a failure and that something must be done. This crisis generally meets with a very poor reception and often precipitates the children's leaving home. Moreover, it is where his daughter is concerned that the father runs the greatest risk of disillusionment. Never considering her as a normal woman, he would like her to remain forever the perfect daughter, and it is very difficult for him to accept the idea that he is no longer the only man in her life.

If a person feels incapable of assuming this exhausting role of parent, it would really be more sensible not to have any children at all or, if children already exist, to have them brought up by nannies and to try to play one's role at least during the school holidays. It must be admitted that the job of being a father at the present time is one of the toughest in the world: he gets no day off and often his only recompense is the satisfaction of a job well done. It is accomplished only by endless patience, an accumulation of details, and a perfectly straight line of conduct.

In order to command, one must first of all know how to obey, and even if modern children seen to reject all forms of obedience, they nevertheless require discipline more than anything else in order to develop into well-adjusted adults.

(See also Paternity)

FEAR

The fear they inspire is as necessary to men as vitamin C in their diets. At home, as at the office, they adore to have people tremble before them and they often confuse fear with respect. Men who are not endowed with natural authority think they have to roar in order to be obeyed. They get what they want, but while they may be feared they are also unloved. Men who know how to command also obtain what they want, but while they may be feared, they are also respected.

If your husband is a roarer, never argue with him and give him the satisfaction of seeming to be terrified, for this is all he seeks; he will soon forget the reason for his outburst and you can then do as you like.

If he terrorizes the children, he runs the risk of giving them lifelong inferiority complexes, and it would be advisable to keep them out of range of his temper. Otherwise, arrange for him to have a heart-to-heart talk with a close friend whom he trusts. But if he is genuinely sadistic and if his greatest pleasure is to see his entourage tremble in fear of him, your only solution is to run away from him as fast as you can.

FIANCÉ

The engagement period may be a glorious time for a young girl, but you cannot say the same for a boy, who always seems a bit embarrassed. The girl shows off her brand-new ring, she busies herself with her wedding plans, makes out invitation lists, decorates the first flat, presents the man of her life to all her girl-friends, who are more or less jealous, and for a few months she is the star of her little set. But the poor boy has to make a good impression worthy of a serious future husband while at the same time he is the butt of tasteless jokes on the part of his friends and colleagues, and he must face up to all sorts of new responsibilities. It must be for this reason that many modern couples eliminate engagements altogether, or at least reduce them to a minimum period of time. There are advantages as well as disadvantages in this custom, since it is, after all, easier to break an engagement than to get a divorce.

Try to make this transition period as easy as possible on your fiancé. Just because you're wearing his ring on your finger doesn't mean that you should suddenly turn into a shrew. Remember that young men are always slightly intimidated by the idea of marriage, and this is not the moment to deprive him entirely of his independence. Even if it means offending Cousin Gertrude or Uncle Albert, don't force him to call on a different member of your family every weekend, but let him suggest the meetings and social events that appeal to him. Try as far as possible to be just the same as you were before you accepted that famous ring.

Some lighthearted young women introduce one man after another as their 'fiancés'; but this type of man, who has already got everything he wants, seldom has any intention of applying for a marriage licence.

(See also Suitors)

FIDELITY

There are many different kinds of fidelity, for more or less valid reasons.

Feminine fidelity may be due to love, education, a

sense of duty, lack of opportunity, or simply force of habit.

Masculine fidelity is based on love for a brief moment, and most often on lack of time.

But neither men nor women can understand the true meaning of fidelity until they have grown old together. (See also Adultery, Affairs, Fifty)

FIFTY

How often we hear of the 'dangerous fifties' and the demon that inflames middle-aged men with juvenile desires! It is true that a fiftieth birthday can be a disagreeable turning point in life, when you have the impression that you must hurry up, that your youth has vanished and when, although you feel as sprightly as ever, your face reveals an age that your heart is not yet ready to accept.

Normal women are generally satisfied simply to dye their hair and get their faces lifted, but men feel the need for young flesh. Husbands who have been perfect until then do not hesitate to cast off their old wives, as they might give away an old winter coat to the Salvation Army at the first sign of spring. They try to maintain the illusion of youth by marrying a woman twenty or thirty years younger than they. There is little one can do to combat this impulse, apart from engaging a good lawyer who will make it ruinously expensive for the husband to get a divorce. At that moment, half of his charm will disappear, and the young woman who had agreed to marry 'a wonderful man, rich in experience and wisdom' – and, needless to add, 'money' – will then hesitate to join her destiny to that of a penniless pensioner. But if he hasn't the faintest idea of divorcing and simply wishes to prove to himself that he is still attractive, you have every interest in giving him a free rein, for he will be only too happy to come home again in order to find peace and perhaps to recover his health, which will probably have been somewhat undermined by the excesses that are really too much for a man of his age.

FIGURES

It goes without saying that the figure is the keystone of all elegance for both sexes. While a tiny woman can be charming when she knows how to accentuate her air of fragility, there is, alas, no salvation for small men – which generally makes them very aggressive. On the other hand, while a heavy woman can at the most be well dressed without ever achieving great elegance, a heavy man, if he is very well groomed, can achieve a kind of majestic allure that comes quite close to elegance. Even a very fat man like Orson Welles did not lack a certain distinction that was a tribute to his tailor. Nevertheless, nowadays men pay almost as much attention to their figures as women do, for although it is relative easy to conceal the beginning and even the full development of a paunch underneath a double-breasted jacket, its presence will immediately be revealed by a pair of bathing-trunks. We simply have to resign ourselves to the glaring injustice of the fact that it takes years of delicious rich food and sedentary life behind a desk or steering-wheel in order for our mates to get fat, but all we have to do is to nibble on a few sweets in order to bulge at least twenty years before they do. However, the jolly fat man is no longer regarded with the same amused indulgence as he used to be before the doctors and insurance companies announced that his days are numbered. And so a loving wife who wishes to keep her husband as long as possible must add to her talents of Cordon Bleu those of a dietician.

If she has married a hopelessly plump little husband who eats cream puffs in secret and gobbles up bars of chocolate the way a slot-machine gobbles up sixpences, he ought at least to pay careful attention to his choice of clothing. Double-breasted jackets are most effective for concealing overweight, but they are not very becoming to small men, who should stick to straight-cut, single-breasted, three-button jackets with long narrow lapels, made up in the most neutral materials possible.

FLESH

Religiously speaking, flesh is the antithesis of the soul, and to make his soul pervade his very flesh is the characteristic of civilized man.

FLIGHT

Napoleon, who didn't retreat so readily from the battle-field, said that the only form of victory in love is flight. As a matter of fact, flight is much more a masculine than a feminine reflex. Even among animals, a female will face a danger that threatens her young, while the male will prudently scamper off to seek shelter.

Women prefer to discuss a problem frankly, even if there is a risk of a painful scene; whereas men dread it so much that they disappear beforehand. So don't be surprised if one day you suddenly cease to hear from a gentleman who had seemed interested in you – he preferred to flee rather than to wipe away your tears!

FLIRTATION

After teddy bears, marbles and cowboy suits comes the game that will amuse your son from the age of thirteen to twenty: flirtation.

Some Saturday evening you will be astonished to see him monopolize the bathroom, when only yesterday you had to nag him into taking a shower. He stays there for two hours, emerging only in order to rush to the telephone. It would be a good idea, by the way, to order another extension immediately, because from now on the telephone will no longer belong to you.

Resign yourself to the fact that your baby has become interested in girls. He is taking his first steps in the direction of manhood and he wishes to appear attractive to the little girls he used to scorn.

Never make fun of him when speaking of his conquests to your friends or even to members of the family. But never make the mistake of trying to become his accomplice by asking him for all the details, because this is an age at which boys are still discreet and particularly sensitive. Aid him financially, but without exaggeration, and give him a little advice on etiquette, for which he will be grateful; you should realize that underneath his air of bravado he's not at all sure of himself. If you meet his little girl-friend and find her ugly and stupid, by all means do not tell him so. Remember that the torments of love at this age are as painful as they are fugitive.

It sometimes happens that even after marriage one partner or the other feels like a youngster again and indulges in a little flirtation one evening. Even if the other one laughs, you should realize that it *never* makes him happy and that he probably won't be in a laughing mood at all when he gets home.

FLOWERS

As a general rule, flowers are the only gift a well-bred woman can accept from a man who is not her husband.

Is he invited out to dinner? He quickly instructs his secretary to send flowers – which will often be charged as a business expense. If the secretary is a woman of good taste, so much the better. But it is more likely that she will play safe by sending a dozen long-stemmed roses or an azalea plant. Men take personal charge of their florist orders only when they are in love or when they feel guilty.

Few men have very good taste in selecting flowers. They usually do not even know the different names and say to the florist: 'I'll take those over there . . .'

If you ever receive flowers of a colour that matches your curtains or upholstery, of the perfect size for the place and the vase you intend to put them in, then the man who sent them is a homosexual with marvellous taste, or else he is madly in love with you.

FORGIVENESS

To forgive is not always to forget; it is, in fact, far more difficult. When you tell your husband, after a grand scene and many tears, that he is pardoned for everything, you are condemning yourself to absolute silence and to the prohibition of the slightest allusion to the lady in question; otherwise, you might as well admit right away that you are incapable of forgiveness.

Men are even less forgiving than we are, although they try to forget as quickly as possible the fact that we preferred another man. What they never forget are their masculine enemies, just as they never pardon a person who has got the better of them in business, even though they know very well that if the positions had been reversed they would not have hesitated to do the same.

On the individual as well as on the national plane, the conquered never pardon their conquerors; they simply watch for an opportunity to revenge themselves.

But what men forgive least easily in others is the role of victims. The more harm one does to a person the more one holds it against him, which is moreover quite natural: how can you be expected to like somebody who has permitted you to be a swindler, a traitor or a perjurer? So never be taken in by the sudden repentance of a person who has really done you harm; he probably thinks it wasn't harm enough and there may be worse to come.

FRIGIDITY

Here is something that a woman should never confess to anybody but her doctor, for no man in the world ever believes that it might be his fault.

GALLANTRY

Gallantry is simply taking the time to be a little bit more polite than necessary, and it is also an agreeably affable turn of mind. There are many more men who are incapable of inventing a well-phrased compliment than men who say exactly what you expect them to say. Maybe the former like you more than the latter, but it is still the latter that you prefer.

If men realized what generous dividends are paid by a little bit of gallantry they would all take lessons in it.

GAMBLER

It is better to marry even an alcoholic than a gambler, for no hospital has yet been willing to try to cure this malady.

If you have the misfortune to marry an inveterate gambler who doesn't know how to stop in time, don't expect that you will be able to make him change his ways. He'll gamble away everything he owns, including his false teeth, and you will end up completely ruined. Give him just one chance, and if he lets you down again leave him as quickly as possible.

GENTLEMAN

The French have borrowed this word directly from the English language as a replacement for *gentilhomme*, which implied a title of nobility. While a gentleman is noble too, his is a nobility of heart and soul. The finest compliment you can pay a man is to consider him a gentleman, and the feminine equivalent is 'lady'. What qualities must one possess in order to merit this title? Qualities which, alas, are disappearing from our habits and morals every day.

> *Courtesy:* A gentleman is more often standing than seated, and he is a good listener.
>
> *Relaxed good manners:* A gentleman is at ease and confident of being welcome everywhere.
>
> *Generosity, but not extravagance:* A gentleman knows the value of every service and doesn't need to overtip in order to attract the attention that is his due.
>
> *Elegance — moral as well as physical:* The 'gentleman gangster' is nothing but a fictitious character in cheap novels.

It is difficult to turn an ordinary man into a gentleman. While most self-made men are rich in other qualities, few of them are authentic gentlemen, for this requires a certain nonchalance and a habit of command that are acquired only by the second generation at the very soonest. The gentleman is a British speciality, like the lawn: both of them have required years of cultivation in order to reach the point of perfection.

And so, mademoiselle, you are mistaken when you claim that you are marrying a certain young man and not his parents, for while there may be a few juvenile delinquents in the best of families, there are even fewer gentlemen among the sons of gangsters.

GIGOLO

The gigolo is a harmoniously proportioned biped, very young, with an underdeveloped brain and doubtful origins. He is generally found in the beds of older women or elderly gentlemen, depending on who is the highest bidder.

In order to avoid the fatigue of a forty-hour week working in an office like everyone else, he prefers to spend at least twice as much time in environments described as 'places of entertainment', where he feeds exclusively on caviare and foie gras. His only ambition is to get married and, by becoming a widower as quickly as possible, to enjoy the advantages of money without the drudgery of earning it. Thus from gigolo he will be able to advance to the much more enviable rank of playboy.

An older woman must really have lost all self-respect

to be willing to pay for the favours of a young man. And she is perhaps the most pathetic and pitiful of all the creatures in the menagerie of The Rich.

GOLFERS

In Anglo-Saxon countries it seems that golf is played mostly by men, for it gives them one more chance to be by themselves, far from household problems. But in France it is rather rare for only one member of a couple to indulge in the sport. Even if you aren't at all attracted by the thrill of driving or the mystery of swinging, you might pay at least one visit to your husband's golf club. After this initiation, you won't be so bored when the man in your life describes his golfing exploits or his misfortune at the bunker of the seventh hole, the miraculous approach he made at the eighth in spite of the huge oak tree and the curve, or Jack Smith's incredible round that is bound to lower his club handicap. Perhaps it would be worth your while to cast an appraising eye on the charms of the lady golfers too!

GOSSIP

Despite their protests to the contrary, men adore gossip. Moreover, they transform their thirst for knowledge into useful business information; and certain more or less confidential publications are nothing more than collections of gossip.

They also enjoy being better informed than their friends, and it gives them status to seem to share the secrets of important people. So never hesitate to tell them what you hear. Even if they do not seem to attach any importance to the infidelities of their best friend's wife, they will be secretly delighted to learn that poor Paul is a cuckold. But while it is nice to amuse them, you should still beware of telling them too much, especially if you haven't verified your story – because quite often a piece of gossip that you consider harmless will be outrageously exaggerated with each repetition and, like a boomerang, it may come back to injure you.

GRANDFATHERS

Perhaps you will be disappointed after reading this book because I haven't given a foolproof recipe for marrying a millionaire; but at least I am going to try to convince you that if you are lucky enough still to have one or two grandfathers, you hold within your grasp one of the most charming of all the men in your life and you should take advantage of the fact without delay.

Modern grandfathers are not very old, but they have sometimes already retired and dispose of unlimited free time which they often don't know how to utilize. You can become their favourite pastime and they can teach you a lot more than your parents who, weighed down by a thousand cares, often have neither the time nor the patience to entertain you. A grandfather is the ideal person to take you (in chronological order) to the circus, to the zoo, to museums, to the theatre, and even on trips. He is an ideal companion on many different kinds of occasions. If he is an epicure (in former times gastronomy was more important than a good figure), he will teach you all about good wine, fine cheeses and countless refined details of the art of living that are completely unknown in our modern snack-bars. If he is a clever handyman, he can teach you various useful arts and crafts that will be an insurance against boredom. If he has lived in the country, he can help you to discover the fascinating world of plants and animals. Since there was less television when he was young, he has had time to read books, and he can sweep you away with him on the magic carpet of literature. Of course, he may be doddery or completely senile, or perhaps simply panic-stricken by your obvious scorn. But even if he is only a former labourer and you are a professor of electronics, there is surely something you can learn from him.

If little girls knew how much they can get out of a grandfather simply by climbing up on his knees, there is a risk that, owing to this precocious experience, they might become fatally irresistible sirens later on in life; and mothers are advised to teach their daughters that the first man they should attempt to win is their own grandfather – by employing, as a matter of fact, the same strategy that is most effective with all the other men in a woman's life: attention and admiration.

'Admire Grandpa!' I can already hear thousands of

sniggering remarks of the order of: 'The old man is much less well educated than we are and he simply doesn't fit into our lives.' This attitude is really shameful, for it is thanks to the hard work of their great-grandfathers that today's young people are able to live as comfortably as they do. Modern scientists, who are flattered, idolized, and provided by the government with fantastic means, are no more than ordinary civil servants compared with the scientists of fifty or sixty years ago, who had to struggle on alone and who, despite their handicaps, made all the great discoveries of the century, which our generation has merely perfected.

Yes, it is really a pity that young people scorn the companionship of their grandfathers. Not only are they thereby losing a marvellous human contact, but when their grandfathers have disappeared, the last traces of a civilization of free and creative individuals will disappear with them, to make way for a standardized, mechanized, conditioned mass society. And it will then be too late to listen to their words of wisdom.

GUESTS

Come now, don't be more charming to the men than to their wives . . .

HABIT

Habit is the chloroform of love.
>Habit is the cement that unites long-wedded couples.
>Habit is getting stuck in the mud of daily routine.
>Habit is the fog that masks the most beautiful scenery.
>Habit is the end of everything.

HAIR

Adam never trained either of his sons to be a barber and so he wore his hair very long, which didn't prevent him from being a very respectable gentleman, despite the fact that he was a little weak with women. According to the era and the latitude, men's hair styles have had their ups and downs.

However, it is curious to note that while all Samson's strength and consequently his freedom, depended on the length of his hair, the moment women wished to assert their independence they started by sacrificing their flowing tresses.

Hair is certainly an attribute of which members of both sexes are extremely fond, since one of the most classic punishments throughout history and even at the present time consists of shaving the heads of criminals and of the conquered. There are, it is true, a few charming bald men who at least have the advantage of seeming intelligent with their high brows, but in general men are very unhappy about losing their hair and there are many more of them than you think who wear wigs.

A loving wife should therefore worry when she notices that her husband's hair is beginning to thin out, and he will be very grateful to her if she gives him massages or buys him appropriate lotions. On the other hand, it would be terribly tactless to bring to her boss's attention the fact that his scalp is starting to show through, and even if you know a miraculous recipe for growing hair, it is certainly not to him that you ought to recommend it. Bald men sometimes seem to enjoy making fun of their little infirmity, but they detest it when other people tease them about the money they save on haircuts – which is, besides, a very vulgar joke.

A gentleman's head of hair really counts for very little in my appraisal of him. The only thing I dislike is a very low hairline that leaves just a tiny space for a forehead, and since I used to be very dark, I naturally prefer blond men – without, however, going so far as to think that only blond men can be handsome. As for men who dye their hair, they are ageing Lotharios, and rather pathetic.

A crew cut gives the impression of an army conscript

when it is worn by a very young man, and of an over-age Boy Scout or a retired colonel when the wearer is not so young. On the other hand, long hair that falls over the eyes at the slightest tilt of the head can make a minor clerk seem as glamorous as a prestigious orchestra conductor, but it is incompatible with the air of respectability required of a company director or a doctor. Nowadays, a man is no longer embarrassed by having curly or wavy hair, but as soon as it starts to get a little thin he should wear it shorter. As for those who 'comb over' – that is, who let the few last remaining strands on the sides grow very long in order to plaster them across the top – they may manage to cover their bald pates, but they also cover themselves with ridicule.

In order to console themselves, bald men spread the rumour that losing one's hair is a sign of virility, and they like to have people think that they lost their own on the field of honour of numerous mattresses. This myth harms nobody, so I don't see why we shouldn't pretend to believe in it. In fact, to make an allusion to it even seems to me to be the best means of helping a man to understand that there is no reason for developing a complex about his baldness, that you would even be grateful to him for being bold as well as bald, and that although you may not be able to enjoy the pleasure of running your fingers through his hair, you are not at all insensible to his charms.

(See also Beards)

HAIRDRESSER

The hairdresser is a very important man in a woman's life, and I know more than one woman who, while flitting from one lover to another with the greatest of ease, thus revealing a most inconstant nature, remains resolutely faithful to her hairdresser, for she gets from him a kind of beauty insurance that no other man can offer her. Nothing changes a woman more than being well or badly coiffured, and the hairdresser therefore becomes a sort of magician to her. Even an all-day beauty treatment transforms her less than does a session at the hairdresser's, and the first piece of advice you can give to a woman who is feeling blue is to rush out and get her hair done.

It is therefore natural for her to feel towards this sorcerer affection and gratitude, which are manifested in the form of tips and confidences small or large.

Queens, princesses and film stars travel with their personal hairdressers, who thus acquire a status equivalent to that of a secretary or a governess, just above a servant; and, like the latter, they are known only by their first names. Nevertheless, they are now received in society to the extent that they have become important businessmen, for they are no longer satisfied simply to curl hair, but have also opened boutiques for selling wigs and all sorts of frivolous accessories capable of tempting a woman who is in a good mood because she is feeling beautiful. They also know all the advantages to be found in exploiting feminine laziness and vanity: parking attendants at the door, upholstered footstools, snacks served under the drier, titles announced in a loud voice, VIP treatment, etc.

Going to the hairdresser's thus represents for most women relaxation, luxury and pleasure. She arrives in a pleasant environment where an entire organization is waiting for her in order to make her more beautiful. In complete confidence she delivers herself entirely into their hands. At last they can talk about themselves, certain not to be interrupted, whereas their best friends only listen to them while waiting for the chance to break in with their own stories.

According to a survey at my own hairdresser's, which isn't a factory like some of the very big establishments but a more discreet salon with a faithful personnel in a fashionable neighbourhood, where the clientele consist more of rich upper-middle-class women who walk over from next door than of frivolous little ladies, this is what they talk about most freely: first of all, their health, then their travels, their parties and finally (because, to repeat, this clientele is upper middle class) the minute details of their intimate lives. 'He likes me to have very long fingernails', etc. The older the woman, the younger is her lover, and the more she likes to brag about him. 'He woke me up in the middle of the night ... he ruined yesterday's style and I simply had to come back this morning.' This sort of thing is common. It's easy to see why the hairdressers and even the manicurists and shampoo girls who hear such examples of idiotic egocentricity for ten hours a day become a little misogynic. If you only knew, my beauties, what your hairdresser generally thinks of you, it would seal your lips forever. And so, next time, try to remember that they too perhaps have a few personal problems. Take an interest in them, or at least refrain from weighing them down with yours as well. You will surely win their esteem.

But if it is you, mademoiselle, who work in a men's barber's shop, and if they entrust to your care their big paws or a head of hair that is all the more precious because it is becoming all the more sparse, I think that you will need to exercise a great deal of patience, for it seems that men also are prone to confessions. However, they are more apt to try to wring your own stories out of you – which they prefer on the spicy side – than to impress you with their own exploits; and while they cannot resist the temptation of bragging a bit too, they are much more discreet about their personal problems.

HANDS

If men knew how much attention we pay to the hands that are going to draw us to them, they would spend all their time at the manicurist's. Of course the best manicurist in the world can never transform the flat, shortfingered hands of a strangler into the fine, long hands of a violinist, or shave off a forest of black hair, or stop the trembling of an alcoholic, or remove the calluses from the hands of a manual labourer and the last trace of grime from those of a mechanic. She can, however, at least file the nails in a rather square shape, push back the cuticle and shine the nails with a buffer – without ever applying nail polish.

A man's character is revealed by his hands. Large, broad, confident hands placed flat on the table: he is calm, sure of himself, devoid of complexes and probably quite kindly; the same hands continually clutching a ruler, a pen or the back of a chair denote repressed power that risks exploding, and probably indicate not so good a character as the first. Fine, nervous hands that delicately caress an object are more likely to belong to an intellectual than to a professional footballer.

Beware of damp hands – they indicate a hyper-nervous individual filled with complexes. I prefer large hands to very small ones, especially if in the latter cases the fingers are white and sausage-shaped. Beware also of hands that are never removed from their pockets by shy men, or the gesticulating hands of a braggart, or the accusing, pointed finger of the sententious, or the clenched fist and white knuckles of the irascible and the tyrannical, or the soft, limp hands of the lazy.

When you marry a man, you place yourself in his hands literally and figuratively, and his hands are there-fore one of the first things you should observe in a future husband.

HAPPINESS

Don't expect any man to bring you permanent happiness every morning on a breakfast tray.

The legs of Marlene Dietrich, the nose of Cleopatra, the voice of La Callas or the fortune of the Vanderbilts are not infallible recipes for obtaining it either, because in that case why should Marilyn Monroe have committed suicide? Why should a millionairess, heiress to an enormous fortune, vainly try everything in order to make life bearable: husbands, lovers, noble titles, drink and drugs? On the other hand, in my Provençal village, why should my dear Titine, who gets up at five o'clock in the morning and goes to bed at midnight in order to keep house for her husband's aged parents, to wash sheets, sheets and more sheets in the depth of winter, out of doors in the icy water of the public laundry trough, to prepare meals for her husband, and to do her housework and mine, always be so cheerful, gay and willing? She has found without realizing it the most precious possession of all: she is happy to be her Mediterranean self, with her alert black eyes, her rapid speech full of good common sense and striking expressions. As a matter of fact, there are certainly more happy people around the Mediterranean than anywhere else; the beauty of the landscape and the gentleness of the climate seem to foster an aptitude for happiness.

But let's see – what exactly is HAPPINESS? It's a frame of mind and a gift from heaven. Just as one painter, like

El Greco or Modigliani, sees the world in elongated forms while another perceives it in terms of splashes of colour, and one creature, like the bee, transforms its nourishment into honey while another, like the serpent, secretes only venom, a human being either knows how to create his own happiness or he doesn't.

Why does humanity seem to like itself less and less, and why does it feel increasingly uncomfortable within its own limitations as it masters the secrets of nature? Is it perhaps haunted by the memory of what happened to Pandora and Icarus?

Since I am merely a very ordinary woman and not a bearded German philosopher, I shall abstain from launching into this debate and shall leave the discussions to learned psychologists on their high lecture plat-forms and to overworked psychiatrists beside their low couches. All I know is that you can find happiness only in the things you do well. A happy marriage is one of these things just as much as a successful career. But there are also little fleeting moments of happiness which are not insignificant at all if you know how to recognize them as they appear and to add them up: a moment of physical harmony, a becoming dress, a perfectly prepared dish, a well-turned phrase, a tiny black seed that is transformed into a big pink flower, a sunny morning and the time to enjoy it, relief from pain, a song you like, an unexpected compliment, a child's damp kiss and a dog's melting gaze, and what else – I know so many of them, large and small, exceptional and everyday, that this could turn into a veritable hymn to life, a song without end.

HEART

I wonder why this rather unappetizing organ should symbolize love, kindness, courage and the very essence of matter?

To tell the truth, one encounters more hearts carved in tree-trunks and portrayed on playing-cards than in the course of everyday life.

HEROES

A hero is a man who forgets to think about himself for five minutes or for a lifetime, and who is prepared to die for an idea or for somebody else.

Women adore famous heroes because they always enjoy a little reflected glory, but they find it more difficult to live with heroes who have remained anonymous. A hero may just as well be a man who throws himself into the Thames to rescue his drowning mother-in-law, or a kamikaze in his suicide plans, or an obscure guerrilla fighter who blows up a train. The more noble and lofty the ideal that inspires a hero, the more difficult it is for a woman to rival such an entity, and she must have a saintly character in order to accept second place in his life.

If your heart is set on marrying a hero, you should

at least share the same ideas, militate at his side, get used to the idea of going to jail, or order your widow's weeds.

HOBBIES

You've married a serious banker whose only pastime is either sticking stamps in an album or decorating all the walls of the house with innocent impaled butterflies. You reach the point where you can no longer stamp a letter without screaming, or you spray tons of DDT in your garden in order to eliminate any trace of these damned lepidoptera. Try to see to it that his hobby remains a harmless pastime and doesn't turn into a devouring passion.

So prepare as many distractions as possible for your husband – social events, trips, etc. – and see that he has as little time as possible to devote to his hobby. He will end up by forgetting it, and the day will come when you can sell his blasted collection in order to pay for your own latest hobby!

HOLIDAYS

Paul Valéry wrote, in his book *L'Idée Fixe*: 'During holidays, everybody makes believe. Some people pretend to be savages, others explorers. Some people pretend to rest; others to exert themselves. As for myself, I make believe quite consciously. The truth is that I try to do nothing at all. But it isn't easy. I know of nothing more difficult. It is a labour of Hercules, a constant preoccupation. I am afflicted with the malady of work. I cannot, I do not know how to do nothing.'

It is certainly true that during eleven months of the year people dream of the twelfth when they can at last do nothing, and most of the time it is with a sigh of relief that they return home at the end of the holiday. If you are very honest with yourself you will admit that often the most wonderful part of a holiday is talking about it afterwards to your friends. Perhaps it is because you have not known how to keep your partner amused and at the same time free. You should realize that it is up to you to organize this period of time between parentheses in the best possible way.

Nothing is more difficult than to change one's rhythm of living from one day to the next, and much of the behaviour that is accepted as natural in the ordinary routine of daily life will suddenly seem shocking during the extraordinary period of a holiday. You are going to have the time for reflection and observation, and while happy marriages return strengthened from a holiday, this is the moment when many tottering unions may hear the bells toll for their lost illusions.

As soon as a family consists of more than three persons it becomes very expensive to stay in a hotel, and in general the solution to the holiday problem is either a rented house or a summer home in the country. In these cases holidays are, for a wife and mother, merely a change of scenery, often to a less comfortable environment where her task is more arduous than ever and where it is even more tiresome than usual to be the servant of the entire family, because they are thinking only of having fun. Painful as this situation may be, you are going to have to organize things so that you suffer as little as possible and at the same time make your family very happy. In a recent poll almost all the husbands replied that the dream of their lives would be to spend their summer holidays as bachelors! Even if you see your husband, already rather portly, standing on his head on the beach in an attempt to impress your daughter's friends, instead of bursting into laughter, try to express your admiration; he will be grateful to you, since you will probably be the only one to do so . . . and this is hardly the moment to remind him of his high blood pressure!

As for the children, let them too do as they like, without, however, forgetting that it is only prudent to keep your eyes open. You can insist that they be home at regular hours if they wish to have their meals with the family, and also that they make their beds and tidy up their rooms. Establish a rotating system for such jobs as setting the table and doing the dishes. Once or twice a week go out to dinner in a restaurant, while the children entertain their friends at home. This will be the moment to try a new hair style or some new earrings – in other words, to make yourself as beautiful and as different as possible, so that your husband will learn to look at you again and even to see you, and so that you will revive a little of the atmosphere of your honeymoon. If you succeed in all this, you will have earned the reward of your holiday.

For young girls this is also a marvellous period of first love and first flirtations; it is the joy of being accepted or the sorrow of being rejected by 'the group', the ambition for some to be the queen of the band, and an apprenticeship in living for all of them. You should, however, warn them that they are more likely to meet disillusionment than future husbands, because for boys the summer holiday is the season for collecting girlish hearts and their interest seldom survives the end of summer. Besides, with the exception of owners of country homes who see each other every year and whose children grow up together from one summer to another, you never know very much about holiday acquaintances, since shorts and outdoor life conceal the social differences which become unbearably apparent once you are back in the city. It is much easier to play a role during the holidays than during the rest of the year, and in fact for many people holiday means a time when they can play the roles that seem to them most enviable. The shy mouse always dressed in grey will finally dare to wear red slacks; the sexually repressed individual hopes to satisfy all his appetites by playing Don Juan; the minor employee at last indulges in the pleasure of commanding, and you see him ordering the waiters around, etc. The choice of a holiday can be very revealing of a person's character and his true personality.

In our occidental world the idea of holidays is increasingly associated with that of salary, and many people would rather have more leisure than more money. But how many of them know how to utilize it intelligently? For many people a summer holiday is simply a rather unpleasant period that has to be survived somehow, because they have become like robots and no longer know what to do with themselves when they no longer receive orders. In a few years there will be so much free time that there is a risk of an immense boredom suffocating humanity. Let's hope that the future Secretary of Leisure, after having exhausted all his projects for the amusement of his fellow citizens, does not as a last resort seek the help of his colleague, the Secretary of the Army – because the greatest distraction of mankind, alas, is . . . war.

(See also Travel)

HOME

Homemaking is a woman's principal task even in this age of equality. It's invariably up to her to decorate it, to give it an atmosphere, a style, a personality that is a reflection of her own. If you have more money than decorating talent, you can entrust the job to an interior decorator – but beware, his results will always be more professional than personal, and even if you enjoy living in impersonal surroundings, you will still have nothing more than a luxury suite in a Hilton Hotel. However, a decorator with a trained eye for measurements and a good staff of workmen can help you to avoid a lot of errors, and if you know exactly what you want and do not let him throw out all your favourite belongings, he can even perform miracles.

In general, men let their wives do as they please with the decoration of their homes, but you should let them organize all the technical jobs such as plumbing, locks, etc., as well as their studies, if they have them.

HOMOSEXUALS

You don't intend to sleep with every man you meet, so why should you eliminate from your life these men who are generally charming, brilliant, sensitive, thoughtful and often very handsome, on the pretext that they are not potential lovers? They are, in my opinion, much more useful than girl-friends. They enjoy gossip as women do, are fascinated by your clothes and by your latest diet. Not the least bit jealous of you as a girl-friend is apt to be, they are much more objective and give you the best advice in the world on everything concerning interior decoration and your personal appearance. Since they don't care to attract attention by being seen only with other men, they will love going out with you (if you are very chic) and your husband need never be jealous. A well-organized woman should always have good homosexual friends as confidants and dancing partners, in addition to her couturier and her hairdresser.

Needless to add, she should never fall in love with one, much less marry one. In spite of all their charms and their sometimes servile imitation of our manners and even of our mannerisms, don't forget that to a homosexual the idea of sleeping with a woman is quite simply disgusting, and while it is possible to cure an alcoholic of his vice, very seldom can any medical or psychiatric treatment cure a homosexual. Some of them, who seem to be 'AC-DC', generally marry only in order to be accepted by society. But it is rather provoking and even humiliating to note that a woman can never succeed completely in recapturing a man who, at one time or another, has preferred a member of his own sex.

HONEYMOON

A honeymoon is a period of time between parentheses, so marvellous that some people cannot bear to see it come to an end, and they prefer to devote the major part of their existence to honeymoons by contracting one new marriage after another.

But, thank heaven, most women haven't this point of view, and when the honeymoon is over, they settle down into true married life in which cares are shared, misunderstandings arise, and habit begins to diminish their earlier ecstasy. Alas, it is impossible to stay the way you were on your honeymoon throughout your entire life, although this would probably be an infallible passport to happiness. But you can at least try this: whenever you are tempted to say something disagreeable or to neglect your appearance or behaviour, just remember that blissful time when each of you thought only of the other.

HOT-WATER BOTTLE

Until the advent of the electric blanket nobody had invented any better substitute for a man in bed.

HUMOUR

Oh, what a marvellous quality! And yet, do you know of a single fairy tale in which the person who has been granted a wish asks for anything apart from riches, youth or beauty, all of which are basically ephemeral?

A sense of humour transforms the most ordinary black-and-white film into a kaleidoscope of colour, and the monotony of daily life into a perpetual pleasure. It prevents people from taking things (and especially themselves) too seriously; it enables you to accept the worst affronts with a smile; it is the most attractive form of courage; and for all these reasons it is one of the most precious gifts in the world. May God preserve us all from people who don't have a sense of humour!

HUSBAND

The first step of every civilized society is to transform the males into husbands. The word still enjoys considerable prestige and is pronounced with a capital H by almost all women.

Before entering into the state of bliss called matrimony, the future husband must win the object of his affections by means of his attractive appearance, his seductive phrases or his bank account – but preferably by all three. However after the honeymoon is over, the husband must begin to think seriously about his material situation, because after having thought only of coming home to go to bed together, his wife begins to notice that life goes on outside the bedroom too, that it is amusing to take part in the fun, but that love requires a more substantial diet than fresh water in order to thrive. Little by little the husband must therefore add to his preceding roles of troubadour, teacher and indefatigable lover those of banker and social leader. It is no longer sufficient for him to charm his wife alone, for she wants to feel envied by all the other women. Since he is also supposed to be her Defender and Protector by the grace of Nature and the Justice of the Peace, he is advised to enrol at a night school in order to learn how to remove a splinter, to repair an electric light, to stop up a leak, to put out a fire and to settle disputes with tradesmen – in other words, to be a doctor, electrician, plumber, fireman and lawyer.

Then he will become a father, and in this role he will be expected to display tenderness, firmness and seriousness, at the same time remaining happy, carefree, full of imagination and fun.

When he reaches the age of fifty it will be most appreciated if he has managed to acquire many honours and a large fortune. He will preferably indulge only in golf – a sport in which it is hoped that he will have a respectably small handicap and will win a maximum of silver trophies. His wife will have become accustomed to his periods of silence, which she will fill (in the best of cases) with the more entertaining presence of the children and of friends of their own generation.

Finally, he is requested not to die too soon, and not too late either, but just at the right moment – in order to leave behind the charming memory of a Perfect Husband.

ILLNESS

Falling ill is abdicating, losing all interest in your usual preoccupations in order to transfer your complete attention to your pulse, your pains and your temperature.

Sacha Guitry wrote: 'A sick man is no longer a man. When a man is sick, he has no name, no age, no fortune, no friends. He has only his temperature. What am I saying? He doesn't even have that – other people have it. As soon as he's got any, they take it away and carry it quickly into the next room.'

If there is a sick man in your house, whether it is your father, husband or son, you may as well cancel all your engagements, settle down next to him in your rocking-chair, and take full charge of operations. Begin by spreading a fine white towel on the bedside table or mantelpiece and arrange on it all the potions and pills the doctor has certainly not failed to prescribe. This will add a note of seriousness to the sickroom and will reassure your invalid by giving him the sense of importance he deserves. Place the telephone in an adjoining room, speak softly, smile and always be there or near at hand.

A sick man is like a spoiled baby who cries when left alone in the dark, and the more domineering he is in normal life the more infantile he becomes when he is ill.

Afterwards, you will perhaps remember the period of his illness as a heavenly moment when you were as indispensable to him as the air he breathed. But don't expect the slightest gratitude from him. He doesn't particularly care to be reminded of his moments of weakness and as his strength returns he will grumble more and more until at last he can return to the office, where he will spend a glorious day describing his malady.

On that same day, follow my advice: make an appointment for a complete treatment at a beauty salon – you will certainly need it!

(See Convalescence)

ILLUSIONS

In many cases women are much more realistic than men, and if they are ugly they try all sorts of artifices in order to make themselves more attractive – whereas men tend to believe that all they have to do is to pay in order to possess us body and soul.

IMPOTENCE

Although it happens to all of them sooner or later, it is the only thing of which they are deeply ashamed.

IN-LAWS

Usually nothing is easier than getting your father-in-law to eat out of your hand. The feat is accomplished in a second if you are pretty, but requires more effort if you are not. And so, according to your means, you are going to have to play up your intelligence or your angelic sweetness.

Brains, common sense and seriousness are bound to please the parents of a rather wild young man. Angelic sweetness will reassure everybody, especially if your mother-in-law is a domineering woman and if her husband has suffered from the fact. In any case you can always start off by telling your future in-laws how handsome you find your fiancé, adding in the very next breath that it is amazing how much he resembles them – the mother's eye and the father's strong mouth and firm chin would be the most flattering distribution of features. Then tell them how much you admire his good manners and congratulate them on having brought him up so well.

As for brothers-in-law, especially younger ones, the thing they will appreciate more than anything else is to be left alone as much as possible. Wait until they too have married before trying to really get to know them.

INSULTS

There are all sorts of insults, and the worst are certainly the least crude. Who has never been called every name in the book by an irate and profane motorist? There are fashions in insults that start in the streets like all other fads.

But street insults don't wound very deeply, except when they are aimed at one's appearance. But if someone is insulted by somebody who knows him well, it becomes terrible. In other words, insults wound only when they contain a grain of truth.

And so the most effective insults are those exchanged at home, where they can attain the summit of cruelty. The worst are not those angry words that escape in a moment of temper but the phrases that are carefully pronounced, after due reflection, and that might even be mistaken for compliments by the uninitiated.

Some couples always have an insult at the tips of their tongues, and they seem to enjoy their little game. But this is a dreadful habit that you should never slip into. And if your husband ever goes so far as to insult you, tell him that you will not tolerate that sort of conduct; leave the house, even if it's dinnertime, and don't return until he has calmed down. Finally, the most effective of all insults is often silence.

INSURANCE

A perfect husband takes out all kinds of insurance, which is why it is advisable to have a perfect husband.

INTIMACIES

There are some intimate details in which men have no interest. So please, I beg you, keep your stories of ovaries to yourself.

JEALOUSY

It seems that among the most common causes of conjugal quarrels, jealousy occupies only the fifth place. But jealousy perturbs more marriages than does actual infidelity because it can be completely groundless: it is a malady.

A woman is born jealous as she might be born blonde. It is even such a primitive emotion that dogs and children are jealous; and jealousy is an expression not only of love but also of possessiveness or envy. Some unhappy people envy the success of perfect strangers, and some women cannot see one of their friends wearing a new dress without turning green.

Sometimes a couple never experience jealousy until the day when one of them realizes that the other has always lied; and nobody can be sure that he will never know this acid, this tumour, this monstrous emotion that drives people to the most terrible deeds. When jealousy settles in a home you can say goodbye to happiness.

Nevertheless, women cannot bear it if their husbands

aren't a little bit jealous, and they go to a great deal of trouble to attract the attention of other men in the belief that this will make their husbands more aware of their charms. It is a double-edged weapon, for it is better to have a husband who isn't jealous enough than one who is too jealous. If, from the day you marry, your husband resents the visits of your friends, don't take the problem lightly, for your entire future depends on your first frank discussion of it. If you give in and stop seeing your friends, he will soon become bored and will reproach you for being anti-social; whereas if you refuse to listen to him but increase your kindness toward him, he will realize that he was mistaken in suspecting you – that is, unless he is Othello in person, in which case I can only offer you my sincere condolences.

JEWELLERY

A man who loves jewels has no alternative but to offer them to his wife. The only ring a man should wear is a wedding ring, and even that should be as simple as possible. All those signet rings set with precious stones should be reserved exclusively for pimps.

Wristwatch straps should never be of metal, but of leather or woven nylon.

Identity bracelets and gold chain bracelets should be packed away in a cupboard. And chain necklaces bearing christening medals are acceptable only along the Mediterranean shores.

So the only jewellery left for our poor men consists of cuff-links, studs (if he has occasion to wear white tie and tails), and perhaps a tie-pin – if they are not afraid of looking like old-fashioned dandies.

JOB

Let's suppose that you have found your dream boss, an intelligent, self-assured, cheerful, affable, fair and generous man in whom you have complete confidence, for whom you are happy to work not only because of the salary he gives you at the end of the month but because, let's face it, you love him – not romantically, of course, but a little bit the way you love your father. Now the problem is to give him satisfaction and not to lose him.

It seems to me that the first quality you need is the ability to perform the job you are trying to land. Certain positions seem brilliant to you and you envy the people who hold them, without stopping to think that they may require certain advantages or circumstances you don't possess, such as the perfect command of a foreign language or facility of speech.

The second indispensable quality: never neglect any detail of your appearance; that is, always be well groomed, well coiffured, well manicured. Unless you are working for the owner of a Soho night-club you should rule out ultra-short skirts, ultra-high heels, ultra-pointed bras under tight sweaters, ultra-blonde, ultra-long hair – in short, everything that is vampish or too high fashion.

Finally, these qualities are just as important as the first two:

– being respectful without being obsequious.

– being punctual but knowing how to accept with a smile a little extra work that keeps you half an hour in the evening.

It is sometimes effective to tell your employer, outside strictly business conversations, how well he looks, or to compliment him on a new suit or an attractive tie, because a boss should always be well dressed. But it is not recommended to overdo the compliments, for it is evident that a litany of praise not only loses all its value but also becomes in the long run increasingly difficult to vary.

It isn't forbidden to be a wee bit in love with your boss, or even to daydream about him if one day during a transport strike he gives you a lift in his smart car and drives you home. A woman who has once dreamed of a man understands him better afterwards. But it is very dangerous, ridiculous and useless to be really in love with him, for he would certainly take advantage of it by asking you to work overtime and to take on all the most tiresome office chores, and he will consider that you are being generously paid for it if he gives you no more than a big smile.

But it isn't forbidden either to ask for a raise when you are sure you deserve it. You must know how to go about it in a businesslike way and never present strictly personal arguments, for you know very well that your boss, wonderful as he may be, doesn't care a bit whether or not you are getting married or changing your flat. But you can point out to him that you are doing more and more of the work in the office, that you are the only one who knows how to handle certain tasks, etc. You should realize that an employer considers all your exploits and sacrifices to be quite normal, and that it is not a bad idea to remind him of them from time to time. But don't be too greedy either, because you are irreplaceable only in your own eyes.

It is nevertheless possible to have a pleasant job without being under the direct orders of your employer, but under those of a department head, and it is obvious that the required qualities are exactly the same, as are the sentimental attachments. Even if your direct boss, who is apt to be younger and an employee himself, owns an old Ford instead of a Rolls, you may eventually want your collaboration to continue during twenty-four hours a day. It is easier to get to know every aspect of the character of a man for whom you work than of holiday acquaintances whom you see only when they are wearing their brightest expressions and their best shorts. There is certainly no better place in which to evaluate the merits of a future husband than in an office. If you are officially an item, it would, however, be in very bad taste to call your boss 'darling' in front of others. But still more ridiculous is the little shopkeeper who speaks of her husband as 'Mr Smith'.

If you have masculine colleagues who hold exactly

the same position in the business as you do, they might develop a certain feeling of rancour and the best way of getting along with them is to ask for their advice rather than to help them with their work. Contrary to what you may believe, only people of superior intelligence are capable of getting any pleasure from work that others have done in their place, and the average employee even has a tendency to defend his functions and prerogatives as a dog defends his bone. It took me years to understand that the entire staff of a large company more or less suspects you of having an eye on their jobs, even when your own is a thousand times more agreeable.

Finally, if you are the director of a company and have men working under you, you will have to exercise a great deal of diplomacy in order to avoid offending them. The worst attitude to adopt is that of the 'outraged princess', but I still think that you should not completely forget that you're a woman, because a successful business-woman has a few advantages over a man and there really is no reason for depriving yourself of them. Why shouldn't you use your charm on customers, competitors and employees? They certainly won't complain. In fact, it is much easier to win the loyalty of men than of women, for the latter are always a little jealous of you.

When I ran my own couture house I employed a number of male cutters and tailors, and the work they did for me was a thousand times more precise, punctual and reliable than that of the women employees. I never gave them orders but always asked them to render me a service, and I cannot remember any one of them ever having let me down.

If you have the choice of working for or employing men rather than women, don't deprive yourself of the men on the pretext that you are a woman; actually, men are much easier to handle. But if you have the possibility of choosing your boss, try to pick one who is very superior to you. Personally, I could never work for a man I didn't admire and who couldn't do anything much better than I. A good boss is a little like 'God the Father' and, as everyone knows, when one is seated at his right hand it is for eternity.

(See also Boss)

JOKES

Private jokes hold a family or a couple together more closely even than blood. Before you pronounce that fateful 'yes', you might add up the hours during which you've laughed together, and if you find only a few minutes, quickly give up the idea of this marriage – or at least postpone it long enough to give the man you love a chance to invent a certain number of jokes for just the two of you. They will provide you with your most enduring memories.

(See also Humour)

KEY

When you have found the right key – the one that opens a man's heart – there is a good chance that it will also open his safe deposit box; it is a master-key.

KISSES

From the peck as impersonal as a handshake to the lingering embrace that climaxed the films of my youth, there is an infinite range of kisses.

Hand-kissing is still a very gracious custom, and I assure you that the glance a man gives you as he straightens up speaks volumes more than if he had pecked you on both cheeks without meeting your eyes. The only kiss to retain any real meaning (which is very often 'yes') is the kiss on the lips, but there are many nuances which I dare not go into here for fear of being accused of writing an erotic manual. Besides, I would surely have nothing much to teach you on the subject.

KNEES

How should a woman react to the knee that touches her own beneath a dinner table? Either you like it or you don't. In the first case, you can blush delicately, lower your eyes and hold your breath, or you can return pressure for pressure and accept the encounter like the sporting person that you are. Both methods have their charm. In the second case, you can say: 'Excuse me, I think I hit your knee by mistake . . .' or, if you are of a combative nature, you can even furiously jab a high heel into the foot of the over-enterprising gentleman. If the incident occurs at the cinema, the best thing to do is simply to change your seat.

LECHERY

Our age is erotic rather than lecherous and would no longer condone such monstrous explosions of sensuality as are seen in the paintings of Hieronymus Bosch. We have become either more civilized or more hypocritical.

LEGS

I leave it to you to imagine what our street scene will look like when men start wearing skirts.

LIBERTY

Total liberty is total solitude. The moment you become attached to another human being, to an animal, or even to an object, you lose a little of your liberty. It is therefore quite ridiculous to believe that you can be in a romantic relationship and at the same time free. And the very fact of being integrated into a society of one kind or another causes the loss of total liberty, because you automatically obey all sorts of rules, fashions, snobbish taboos, the pressure of other people's opinions, traditions, etc.

It seems that liberty is to be found in work. In a certain sense, perhaps it is. But in the immediate moment, work is more like slavery.

So we are satisfied with a supervised liberty that many peoples envy, but since God chased man from the Garden of Eden, he is still only relatively free.

Women are terribly proud of having won their independence and having legally shaken off the yoke of masculine authority. In reality, they do not know very well how to utilize this liberty and it will take some years for them to find the perfect balance between emancipation and enslavement. In their hearts, women dream more often of love than of liberty.

LIES

In order to differentiate between truths and lies, one must first have a very clear idea as to what exactly is the truth. To 'call a cat a cat', as our saying goes, is not so easy, according to the affection you happen to feel for this animal, because a dreadful Tom and an adorable kitten are both cats, just as the same story related in good faith by ten different witnesses results in ten different stories.

At least half our contemporary habits are designed to camouflage the truth, from up-lift bras to tinted foundation creams. All the newest materials are imitations –

some of wool, others of silk, still others of leather, marble or wood – in fact I don't know of any which has an identity of its own. As for advertising, which promises passion and romance to women who use a certain washing powder – let's be charitable and not develop the subject any further! In short, we live in a world of lies and it is only natural that our behaviour should be affected by the fact. All social life is based on etiquette, which is nothing but a permanent lie.

At what point then does it become a sin to tell a lie? When it is slanderous, or when the lie is told with the intention of causing harm? Certainly, but also when an unnecessary truth can only wound. What is the good of revealing to the man who loves you that you have had x lovers, that the little son whom he adores is not his own, that you hate his mother, that you only married him for his money, etc. – is it to ease your conscience? Nonsense. If you do it, it can only be with the intention of making him suffer. You say with an innocent air that you don't know how to tell a lie. As a matter of fact, lying does require a certain amount of imagination and a good memory. All right then, instead of causing harm with painful truths, since you are no good at acting, you can start by never doing anything you cannot freely talk about.

Some people are such good liars that they even lie to themselves. Perhaps they are thus less bored than other people, and perhaps it is an easy way to avoid being too unhappy. I once knew a charming woman who, when she bought herself a sheepskin coat, wrote on the stub in her cheque-book which nobody else would ever see, since she was a widow: 'For Beaver Coat.' During the war this same woman used to serve ordinary packaged biscuits and call them 'petits fours', and she said that her son-in-law owned an 'enormous' Peugeot 403 (the Peugeot company would surely have been interested to learn that its assembly-line cars could thus increase in size at the buyer's will!) Although it inspired smiles this obsession caused no harm to anyone, and it even became a sort of heroism for, when this same lady died of cancer after horrible suffering, she pretended until the very end that she was unaware of the imminence of her death, in order to avoid painful scenes. The lady was my mother.

While all truths may not be good to tell, childish lies are simply stupid and as such they do nothing to make life any easier. You've burned a hole in your husband's beautiful shirt? Dash out and buy another one instead of placing the blame on a faulty iron. You've broken the ashtray he was so fond of because it was a gift from his pals in the Artillery? Tell him about it at once, show him how terribly sorry you are – but don't add that it was an awful eyesore anyway. And don't balance the broken fragments together in the hope that he will make it fall himself. Train your children to tell you about all the little damage they have done, and punish them only if they conceal it.

In my profession I have learned that it is better business to tell the truth than to tell a lie, for the woman whom you have outrageously flattered will eventually find herself face to face with her mirror, her husband, and especially her girl-friends, and the latter will certainly not hesitate to tell her that at her age she looks ridiculous in an apple-green miniskirt. Personally, I am always distrustful of commercial or feminine compliments, and the only one that is worth anything to me is the long, uncompromising stare that takes in every detail of what I am wearing. The day I no longer receive that, I shall retire to the South of France, I shall eat cakes all day long, and, like Madame de Castiglione, I shall veil all my mirrors.

LIFE OF THE PARTY

It is useful to know a few of them in order to animate social gatherings; but you should realize that, like clowns, they are generally gloomy in private. This is a type of man who should be seen only in public and who ought to remain a bachelor.

LISTENING

Voltaire wrote: 'The way to the heart is via the ear.' How often have you been told that you must listen to what is being said to you instead of merely pretending to listen? And yet I realize that most of the time conversations are merely noises that we hear without registering them.

Whenever I find myself drifting into an internal

refuge and when the hubbub of conversation is no more comprehensible to me than Japanese, I force myself to come back to earth, so that even some idiotic twittering creature who may not teach me anything will at least like me.

It is not within every woman's power to be beautiful, elegant and seductive, but anybody can be attentive; and since this is a major asset in getting ahead, why deprive yourself of it?

LOVE

If there is one theme that I approach with the greatest humility, it is certainly this one, for while I don't presume to have anything new or even very intelligent to say on the subject, neither do I wish to get around the difficulty with a witty phrase or a pirouette.

Love can mean so many things . . . a feeling of omnipotence, of fulfilment, of bliss, which finally dispels the oppressive sensation of solitude that everybody feels in a crowd. But love, when you have lost it, can also be complete and hopeless despair. Some people never experience love; and some confuse it with a great many other things . . .

Why do certain human beings never love anybody at all, or never even inspire love in anybody else, not even in their parents? This is perhaps the gravest injustice in the world, for which society will unfortunately never find a remedy. And that is why we should regard with pity rather than with scorn all those blind souls who grope along in what is customarily referred to as vice – liquor, drugs or sexual debauchery of all kinds – for they are desperately seeking the most precious gift that God has given to his creatures: love.

LOVERS

Technically, a lover is a gentleman who enjoys the favours of a lady who is not his wife, but during the eighteenth century the word was employed mostly in the modern sense of 'beau' or 'suitor'.

However, the gentleman beside whom you stretch out in bed or on the back seat of a car as casually as you'd take one last drink hasn't the right to be called your lover, because the word is gradually regaining its former value and quality, and once again designates a superior category of men who are loved.

The true lover belongs to a race that is fast becoming extinct, for in order to exercise his talents he must have time as well as imagination. A lover worthy of the name will not start by taking your breath away as he presses you tightly to him while dancing, but he will make you laugh by telling you amusing stories. He doesn't have to make you drink in order to make you lose your head, because the little spark in his eyes will intoxicate you much faster. He doesn't need to take you shopping in the West End, because you will be just as happy to receive some witty object he discovered at the Flea

Market. And he will never bring you anything as banal as long-stemmed roses or a box of chocolates, but the smallest bouquet of violets will be accompanied by a marvellous letter.

Finally, a true lover exercises as much imagination in bed as he does in everything else, and even if he falls asleep afterwards it will be in your arms. A lover is never a snoring back.

The ideal lover is a person whom you help to create something, whom you inspire, who immortalizes you on canvas or in a book. How far removed we are from the back seat of a car parked in some shady lane! So, my pets, I advise you to seek your lovers in universities rather than in gymnasium dressing-rooms – although there are undoubtedly a few football players who write poetry and a few philosophers who think of nothing but their meals. In any event, wherever and whenever you find this rarity – a lover – try to turn him as quickly as possible into a husband.

(See also Beau, Boy-friends, Fiancé, Suitors, Sweethearts)

LUCK

I believe that the best formula for attracting good luck is contained in the phrase: 'Heaven helps those who help themselves', whereas I am rather sceptical of the French adage: 'Luck strikes while you sleep.' Embittered people are apt to say enviously that 'So-and-So has had a lot of luck', without ever considering that he may simply have known how to take advantage of his opportunities by 'striking while the iron is hot'.

A person who is convinced that he was born under a lucky star can always try to win the Irish Sweepstakes; personally, I have more faith in the results of hard work.

If you hesitate to unite your destiny with that of a young man who continually complains that he's un-lucky, you should give him added proof of his conviction by dropping him as fast as possible.

MAN

In recent times it hasn't been easy to 'be a man' in the traditional sense, since it required an attractive mixture of authority, virility, a sense of duty and justice, tenderness at home and firmness at the office; and he also had to give an impression of strength, to be the provider for his family, to have the courage to fight for an idea and to die for his country. In compensation for all these obligations – or perhaps because of them – men ruled over their wives and their wives obeyed them – or at least pretended to, since women at that time had to obtain by charm and ruse what they later obtained by legislation.

After centuries of uncontested superiority men eventually accorded almost equal rights to women and during the past fifty years they have grown accustomed to seeing women perform the same activities as they. All this was still quite tolerable and they were reasonably well adjusted to the change. They dried the dishes and sometimes gave the baby his bottle, but the family income was twice as large as before, and even if they were sick there was generally no longer a prospect of certain penury. Men retained a semblance of authority and they were still the masters in bed.

Then the Pill was invented, and women experienced true independence for the first time. Moreover, having acquired new techniques (mostly from books), they now challenge men to prove their virility, and there is an immense gulf for modern men between the position of imposing their law, like our grandfathers, and of receiving orders, like our sons. Modern women insist that men provide them with sexual satisfaction, scorning those who fail in this endeavour. They demand equal rights, but they still want a priority card when they are pregnant. In other words, what they demand is even more than equality; it is privilege plus protection.

So what is the meaning of 'being a man' to modern women? How can a man be a master and an equal at the same time? How can he be the sole provider as well as forty-nine-per-cent partner? How can he be a conquering lover and a piece-work labourer?

We shall finally demand so much that unhappy men may one day disappear from the face of the earth, like other creatures in whom women have taken too great an interest – such as Somali leopards and birds of paradise.

MANNERS

It sometimes happens that a woman marries a wonderful man who has very bad manners. While one can reprimand children for certain bad habits (which, moreover, should not be permitted to degenerate into habits), it is not so easy to correct adults in the same way. The best method is probably to broach the subject in a teasing way, or to impose a fine of a kiss, for example, each time your husband picks his teeth in public.

It would probably be possible to estimate how long people have been married from the degree of courtesy they practise in private. If both partners possessed sufficient strength of character to maintain on all occasions the same good manners as when they were engaged, many a divorce would be avoided. It cannot be repeated too often that married love can be slowly strangled to death by the sight of hair curlers, the absurdity of snoring, and repulsive table manners.

In the long run, slovenliness or indecency becomes unbearable, and good manners should be placed right after love as the best recipe for an enduring, happy marriage.

MARRIAGE

I may as well admit right away that, confronted with the problem of discussing such an important subject as marriage in a few pages, when a marriage takes two entire lifetimes and a great deal of effort to create, I should prefer to describe a dinner party in Tibet – where I have never once set foot. Few people would be able to contradict me, whereas on the subject of marriage everybody has his own ideas and personal recipes.

By getting married a woman admits that she needs a man to help her live her life. However, she should be reasonable enough to realize that, while there is no limit to what she can ask of herself, if she hasn't the courage to live alone she must divide her ambitions in two and not demand too much, since her husband cannot be everything, including herself. Many a woman gives the impression that the successful capture of a husband was the one great effort of her life and from then on he is expected to take care of everything. He will carry her across the Red Sea in his arms and perform the daily miracle of smoothing out all life's little problems. This breed of strong men is, unfortunately, in the process of extinction, and a more accurate illustration of modern marriage would be a man and a woman walking hand in hand, rather than one carrying the other.

For many women marriage also means social position, and in order to acquire this façade they are willing to pay the price in private; otherwise, how can you explain the fact that ugly old rich men always manage to marry young and pretty girls?

A successful marriage, however, is none of these things; neither is it a mating or a partnership, but nevertheless a little of both, because everyone knows that a marriage can be really successful only when there exists a moral as well as a physical harmony between the two partners.

If the premarital 'trials' that are nowadays customary among young people didn't lead so often to forced marriages owing to pregnancy, one could only applaud this system, for it is appalling to think that on the evening of a ceremony to which friends and relative have been invited from far and near, and over which a vicar or priest has presided, there remains the possibility that at first contact these two newlywed bodies may give each other goose flesh.

Physical compatibility alone is not sufficient to assure a durable marriage. The first quarrels are patched up on the pillow, but since this accessory is soon returned to its original function of facilitating sleep, there remains in the morning the bitterness of reproaches and of mutual misunderstanding. If two fiancés, drawn together by physical attraction alone, have not taken the time between kisses to discuss their respective tastes, their future ambitions, or even to describe their childhood, they run the risk of marrying a stranger whose gestures are understandable but whose language is not. The elation of the first few days cannot last an entire lifetime. Even fireworks becoming boring after a while. But it is not for lack of them that a marriage isn't marvellous – on the contrary. Months and years of happy hours one after the other are far more beneficial and difficult to achieve than a few moments of frenzied passion inevitably followed by a period of depression.

Successful marriages may be built on a series of mutual concessions, but you can become very tired of climbing the nearest mountain every Sunday with a pack on your back if you have tender feet, or of listening to Schoenberg if you only like Sinatra. So if you haven't exactly the same tastes at the beginning, you must either acquire them or resign yourselves to enjoying your distractions separately – which very often happens at the end of a few years, but which is not the goal to seek at the very beginning. This is the explanation for the well-known preference of intelligent men for empty-headed women, who they can model to their tastes more easily than women with ideas of their own.

Perhaps you can tell whether a marriage has been successful or not only when it has reached its Golden Anniversary. If, after the ecstasy of the first few months, the two partners have shared the joys of success and the pains of failure, if each has thought more of the other than of himself (which might be one of the definitions of love), if children have been a happy extension of their love without monopolizing the affections of one parent or the other or, on the contrary, having been the subject of dispute, if the sound of your husband's key in the lock day after day has invariably given you a little wave of pleasure, then – but only then – can you pride yourself on having made a happy marriage.

MARRIAGE (OF REASON)

Humanity is endowed with so little reason that there is always a somewhat pejorative insinuation when we speak of a 'reasonable' action. But just try to explain to romantic youth that the best outcome one can expect from a marriage of love is an eventual transformation into a marriage of reason, and that to be reasonable means not only to make the best of things, but also to think intelligently;

– that very often love is merely an organic phenomenon, whereas reasoning is an intellectual activity limited to human beings;

– that two people stand a much better chance of finding happiness when they share the same tastes, the same ambitions and the same education, even if they may not feel any world-shaking passion for each other;

– and that in any case world-shaking passions don't last very long and leave a terrible void.

So try to explain to young people that affection, esteem, companionship, and pride in the name one bears, are worth much more than a few thrilling nights. *You* try it . . . I certainly wouldn't dare to!

MASTER

Women say they no longer want one at any price, and yet most of them seek one desperately.

ME

This particular word should be forgotten on the steps of the church in which you have just been married.

MECHANICS

Men are convinced that women understand nothing about cars and mechanics; it would be worth while taking a few lessons and learn the barbarous names of the different parts of a car engine if only to see their reaction! In fact it would be much less difficult than it is to become a doctor or a lawyer, and it would impress them much more.

A woman who consults a mechanic is always in a position of inferiority, and I wonder if this isn't one of the few remaining trades in which men have no need to fear the menace of feminine competition. Have you noticed their air of assurance when they do no more than raise the bonnet of the car? And they pronounce a definitive diagnosis with the authority of a Nobel Prize-winning surgeon.

All things considered, I think it would be wiser and certainly more comfortable for us to let them have their dear mechanics all to themselves, don't you?

MENTAL CRUELTY

Mental cruelty is a polite form of hatred. It is a game that is usually played at home, where everyone knows each other's weak points well enough to be able to make the most cutting remarks.

You can kill somebody by distilling nastiness day after day almost as surely as you can kill him by slipping a few drops of arsenic into his coffee.

MERCENARY

All men try to dazzle the women they hope to conquer, some with a racing stable, others with a bank account, others simply with a flashy car or the security of a government pay cheque. But none of them ever promises us eternal love, spiritual communion or poetry in our daily lives. Nevertheless, men complain that women are mercenary, while the truth is that they are the ones who talk only of money. The day when riches are no longer the number one goal of men, women can afford to be foolishly unmercenary.

MILLIONAIRES

Let's speak frankly: there are more millionaires whom you would be afraid to find at the top of a coconut tree if they were let out at night than millionaires who look like Brad Pitt, and yet they have all the women they want.

I too have dreamed, while drifting off to sleep, that I met a millionaire who immediately spread at my feet a rug of Somali leopard embroidered with emeralds, on the deck of a three-masted yacht anchored in the Bay of Acapulco (or perhaps on a desert island, since the greatest luxury at the present time is solitude). Only in my dream he looked like a film star, sang like Sinatra and talked more of love than of oil wells. But when I have been wide awake I have seen some real live millionaires who were definitely less attractive, and before whom charming young women seem to swoon in ecstasy, as if a cheque-book could take the place of a heart, sex appeal and intelligence. I have nothing but admiration for these women because, believe me, to win and hold a millionaire and to extort his worldly goods isn't an easy job.

The least dangerous type of millionaire is the kind who still works, because he leaves you at least forty to forty-five pleasant hours a week. But those who impose their presence twenty-four hours a day are generally not worth all the trouble these ladies take over them – unless the family doctor has guaranteed that they haven't long to live, because the only really enviable relationship with a millionaire is to be his widow.

Perhaps all this is nothing but sour grapes. Perhaps I would, after all, prefer a 20-carat blue diamond ring to my freedom of mind; perhaps groves of orange trees in the South of France and a Roman palace decorated by Michelangelo would knock me for a loop and suffice to make me happy. I really don't know, for the situation has never arisen. What I do know is that whenever I meet a millionaire, attractive or otherwise, I am absolutely paralysed by fear lest he believe my friendliness is inspired only by the attraction of his fortune. And therein lies the personal tragedy of millionaires: many unmercenary people are too inhibited to become their friends.

However, after observing a number of women who were quite frankly out to bag a millionaire, I think I can define the necessary qualifications of a perfect gold digger. She should:

– be at least twenty years younger than he: millionaires like them young;

– have had several famous husbands or many well-known lovers: millionaires like well-tested values which have been highly publicized;

– be infinitely patient in all circumstances: millionaires are often capricious;

– listen raptly to their every word: millionaires like to received undivided attention;

– always laugh at their jokes: millionaires like to think they are witty;

– be wide-eyed with admiration: millionaires are not always as sure of themselves as they seem;

– behave as often as possible with disarming naïveté: millionaires need a rest from the people they see during business hours, and those people are very far from being naïve;

– have an unquenchable passion and thirst for earthly goods, an adoration for the Golden Calf so constant and unwavering that you never lower your glance from its gleaming image, an iron will and a single goal: MONEY.

Good luck!

MIRROR

There are as many men as women who are in love with their own image – but the former are even less easily forgiven for it.

MISALLIANCE

As long as men still give their names to the women they marry and a shepherdess can become a princess from one day to the next, there is no misalliance – unless the princess marries a shepherd and thereby loses her title. The prince involved in a misalliance of this sort is the hero dearest to the hearts of shopgirls, whereas a woman who does the same merely inspires pity and scorn.

It will take a long time for women to overcome this particular form of inequality.

MISERS

Oh, what an ugly vice is avarice! And how stupid it is to love money for its own sake! A miser is stingy not only with his money but also with his feelings, and to marry a miser is to prefer one's purgatory on earth. If this misfortune has befallen you, and if you feel trapped like a fly in a spider's web, the only way to free yourself – apart from divorce or murder – is to get a job and to spend your earnings on yourself and your children. If you succeed in sneaking some of the food money or in cheating in your household accounts, and even if you are unfaithful to your miserly mate – all I can say is: 'Good for you!'

MISTRESS

There are several different cases of a mistress:

That of the married woman who has an unmarried lover. This is the most classic situation, in which, to facilitate matters, the lover is also the husband's best friend; theoretically, it is a secret affair, and if the lover has the same working hours as the husband, the clandestine meetings are not very easily arranged.

The case where both lovers are married to other people. These 'false marriages' are quite common in the wealthy strata of society, so you must be very careful when you send out invitations to a large party in order to avoid a blunder; even if you have met the husband of a lady with somebody else's wife, it is not advisable to invite the four of them at the same time; these false couples sometimes last a lifetime and are, when you come to think of it, neither more nor less blameworthy than if they had divorced in order to remarry.

The case of the unmarried woman who is the mistress of a married man is certainly the least agreeable for the woman, who always has the impression of getting the crumbs from a feast.

Finally, the case of two unmarried people who live together no longer shocks us.

Despite our more liberal morals – or, if you prefer, our less puritanical outlook – there is still only a very tiny minority of women who do not prefer the title of 'Mrs' to that of mistress, even an 'official' one. And a married man who takes a mistress must have a very special character in order to enjoy being caught in the middle between two jealous women!

(See also Adultery, Affairs)

MONEY

The entire life of every inhabitant of this planet – except perhaps for Buddhist monks – is completely centred around on thing: money. To underdeveloped peoples, money simply means the difference between eating one's fill and going hungry; but to the rest of us it is the very foundation of civilization, for without money there would never have been any artists or scientists, or any possible progress. So we may as well admit right away that money is our major preoccupation (after health, of course), and almost all the relationships we form with others are concerned with it in one way or another. Even the expression 'to earn a living' is full of implications because, since God chased Adam and Eve from Paradise, man can enjoy the gift of life only on condition that he work in order to merit it. Formerly, this privilege (?) was reserved for men, leaving women no means of acquiring money apart from marrying a rich man; and since marriage entailed additional expenses for the husband, it was customary to provide brides with a dowry. Venality is therefore not an exclusively feminine fault, as people tend to believe. In fact, if dowries had never existed and if all the ugly but rich maidens had thus been eliminated from reproductive activity, I wonder if the human race would not be far handsomer than it is.

Although money may not automatically bring happiness and love, nobody apart from a real hypocrite would refuse to admit that money certainly helps to inspire these sentiments and that it remains the most widespread means of seduction by men on every level of society. However, it is a very curious fact that men prefer to be loved for qualities for which they are in no way responsible, such as good looks or intelligence, and that they never willingly admit to having been loved for their financial success, of which they are nevertheless extremely proud.

You have to be terribly young to believe that love can withstand poverty indefinitely, and the only excuse for marrying a poor young man is the belief that he is so intelligent and hard-working that he will not remain poor for very long.

While richness and poverty are in no case criteria for judging men, since many rich men are stupid and hateful and many geniuses are penniless, it is still true that it is much easier to cultivate one's intellect or to practise charity when one is not completely preoccupied with earning enough money to pay for the next meal.

With married couples, money problems are often a poison that slowly destroys their union. After having married for love in the most romantic way, a young woman who is harassed by household chores and a not very lucrative outside job cannot avoid comparing her life with that of her old friends, and she will begin to reproach her husband for his modest income. The vision of the beautiful dress she would so love to be able to buy will expand in her dreams until it overshadows all the fine qualities of the man she chose to be her husband, and the poor fellow will start to run into debt in order to satisfy her, or simply in order to have a little peace. The bills to be paid each month will dance a saraband in his head all night, and he will work like fury in order to meet them (his employer, moreover, counts on this added incentive). But as his salary increases, so do the needs and desires of his wife and, in the best of cases, he will find himself completely worn out at the end of his life, having finally satisfied all of his wife's wishes but having sacrificed in the process the gaiety or sense of fun that was his most charming quality and, in fact, the very reason why she married him.

Men who grumble all the time about the thoughtless way their hard-earned money is being thrown around should stop to consider. Women have gone to work not only because they are bored at home but also because the money they earn themselves has a sweeter flavour than the money they used to have to beg for every day. The prestige of the traditional 'family provider' has virtually disappeared, but I hope for his sake that there will always be women who prefer to play the game of feminine seduction rather than to work. As a result of the present situation, the era of kept women has practically disappeared; while a man can deduct from his income-tax the members of his family and even alimony payments to ex-wives, the income tax collector controls private morals together with the nation's revenue by adamantly refusing to deduct the running expenses of a mistress.

The only pleasant way of handling family money questions is for the husband and wife to collaborate completely.

Men have only themselves to blame if women always seem to be asking for more, because they are the ones who like to let it be known that they are lavish spenders, and that the best way of getting money out of them is to take them at their word. 'With such an important position as yours, the least you can do is to offer me a sable.' It works every time.

If your husband insists on assuming the role of treasurer, which, it is true, endows him with his last remaining vestige of authority, the only thing left for you to do is to play the little game, far too strong a term for all the little ruses, the little white lies, the little daily servilities to which the most honest of women are obliged to resort in order to justify certain expenses. But if you are brutally honest with yourself, it is still prostitution.

I cannot remember who it was that said: 'Life is wasted in the process of earning a living.' It must be admitted too that money distorts almost all human relationships.

MONOGAMY

An instinct for monogamy would seem to exist only in certain species of wild animals, because no domestic animal possesses it and it is a very difficult habit to inculcate in human beings. It has even been necessary to punish the crime of polygamy by religious and civil laws, in order to prevent its practice on a large scale.

But perhaps more effectively than laws, the expenses of a harem are enough to deter an average wage-earner from imitating the extravagant customs of oil-well owners in Bahrein.

MOTIVES

When a person picks a mate or lover the choice is never based on love alone.

The motives are not the same for men as they are for women.

Men are motivated by:

– boredom
– vanity
– instinct for the chase

- a love of comfort
- the need of a spring tonic
- the desire to perpetuate their names
- determination to keep their land or fortunes in the family

Women are motivated by:

- boredom
- a desire for security
- money
- a spirit of contradiction
- a spirit of imitation
- laziness
- reproductive instinct

MUSCLES

Personally, I prefer wit. In general, a man retains his wit until the day he dies, whereas his muscles . . .

MUSIC

If you don't have the same taste in music, I hope your home is a very large one!

MYSTERY

If women knew how much they are losing by unveiling all their charms, they would hurriedly don ankle-length dresses again.

Mystery was more becoming to them, and it must be admitted that certain forms of nudity are enhanced more by dim lamps and intimacy than by the full light of day. Then, too, why should men pay to see what is blithely flaunted under their noses every day?

Men do not like *too* much mystery either, and they run away from the woman who always has a finger on her lips and an air of conspiracy. Beautiful spies have more success in films than in real life. A little touch of mystery is intriguing to men, but too much of it scares them away.

NEW

It's a woman's reason for buying clothes.
  It's a man's reason for falling in love.

NIGHT

Before and at the beginning of married life, we wait for night to come as if it were the embarkment for Cythera; but afterwards night is too often a time for snoring and hair curlers.

NUDITY

Don't reveal too much if it isn't absolutely flawless; thus, when he discovers imperfections it will already be too late.

OATHS

Although young people lightheartedly engage their seemingly unlimited futures by vows which they believe to be eternal, older people hesitate to gamble the little time that is left to them, which is not a very logical situation. An oath is a sentimental contract with no retraction clause; it is also a solemn promise that one has told the truth. Some people swear about anything at all on the heads of those who are dearest to them, whereas others are taken at their word without their having to do so much as raise a hand or spit upon the ground. In both senses of the word – as a promise and as a truth – you should make only one or two oaths in your entire lifetime: they would then retain all their value.

ORDERS

The first requirement of an order is to be clear; the second is to be politely phrased – in other words, to bear the least possible resemblance to an order.

OUTDOORS

From time to time even the most sophisticated women should know how to camp in a tent and to forget about their make-up and high heels. Even though you may be happy only at the Ivy, you must know how to slip into an old pair of blue jeans and to go on a picnic. And if they say that you are 'a wonderful sport', believe me, it's well worth a couple of bramble scratches or the close-up view of a few red ants.

OVERDO

In business, as in love, exaggerated zeal is very tiring. An over-zealous employee is always a little disquieting, and I am enormously distrustful of obsequious servants. Whenever somebody overdoes things or is over-attentive, it is because he wants something from you, even though you may not be able to imagine what. Even in social life I am slightly repelled by a person who is too amiable, and if someone absolutely insists on seeing me all the time, it only makes me want to run away. The law of supply and demand governs all human relations, and the more you advertise your interest the less people will feel like inviting or liking you.

PARTIES

A party should be lively, but it shouldn't degenerate into an orgy. You must therefore know the exact alcoholic capacity of each of your guests, and instead of insisting that they drink another whisky, offer them a glass of orange juice. It is desirable to bolster the morale of poor, hard-working men who return exhausted from the office by giving them their favourite drink five minutes after they arrive; afterwards you can give them a second one. But if you serve wine (which is less harmful) with the dinner, they will be brilliant until the end of the party, whereas they often end up by falling asleep if they have been uproariously high at the beginning of the evening. As for the man who discovers a sudden and spectacular passion for his neighbour's wife, make him change his place or openly tell him to behave himself.

Unless, of course, you would like it to be said that things happen at your parties which ... Well, in that case, put out the lights and scatter cushions everywhere, have a selection of soft music or, on the contrary, the latest 'pop' records in order to drown out the other noises, but above all don't look at yourself in the mirror when you have to turn on the lights again!

PARTNERS

Your husband's business partner is a man who has sufficient confidence in him to become associated with him; he believes that your husband's qualities will compensate for his own weaknesses, or that their combined efforts will lead them to success.

This man, as well as his wife, holds a special place in your life. Although they may have the same business interests as you, they may not have the same tastes, and they may not have the same social background as you. In this case you should invite them alone and not attempt to mix them with your own friends, which might embarrass everyone concerned; but you cannot avoid inviting them to formal ceremonies such as weddings and christenings.

It is also possible that you may not feel the slightest friendliness toward your husband's partner's wife. If so, by no means show it: business is business!

PASSING FANCY

A passing fancy used to be an exclusively masculine pastime; the fire blazed for a few days and went out as quickly as it had started. Now woman can also indulge in passing fancies without attracting ostracism, but they still find it a little difficult to begin an affair which they themselves intend to abbreviate.

Nevertheless, nobody has yet invented anything better than a passing fancy for passing the time.

PATERNITY

The birth of a baby is like an earthquake that upsets all married couples' habits. From being turbulent children and carefree lovers, they are going to have to move all at once into the camp of the 'old married couples', and I think that this little revenge must contribute a bit to the obvious delight of the future grandparents, who at last see the hour approach when their restless progeny must settle down, finally caught in the grips of all the problems which they have had to solve before them.

While it is the young woman who has to undergo almost all the inconveniences of a pregnancy, it is odd to note that she usually bears up under this transformation better than her husband. While she has the feeling of a mission that fills her with secret jubilation, he only sees her changed appearance and the lissome partner of his amorous games seems to have become a staid and matronly stranger. The notion of paternity is not a natural instinct, and although a few beasts like the lion and almost all kinds of birds nourish their mates and offspring for a while, domestic animals are only interested in procreating all over the place without the slightest concern for the consequences. I should very much like to have a naturalist explain to me this difference, for the fundamental nature of the human male seems to be closer to that of these animals than of the civilized patriarch who nourishes and protects his little family and toils throughout his entire life in order to leave it an inheritance. What is accepted as paternal instinct in our civilizations is probably nothing more than a manifestation of masculine pride which causes men to wish to perpetuate their names and to rule over a tribe.

The feelings which stir the heart of a future father are therefore very contradictory: depression at the thought of so many new responsibilities, pride in founding a lineage, astonishment in face of the changes in his wife; and even if he feels caught in the trap of life, society requires him to put up a brave front, so he assumes before the world the necessary air of solemnity.

All the women in the family, including his own mother, are going to band together and he will discover with a certain degree of horror the terrifying phenomenon of feminine solidarity. As soon as the baby is born, that 'moist and screaming thing', as François Nourissier describes it, usurps the priority which he had always theretofore enjoyed, and he feels superfluous. It is not surprising that, thus dethroned, he attempts to resume his bachelor habits or, in the best of cases, shuts himself away with the television.

If his wife is not very careful, the first mortal misunderstandings are going to insinuate themselves between herself and her husband. It is at this moment that her true destiny – mother or wife – will take its shape, for it is extremely difficult to be both in absolutely equal proportions, and certain women, even though they are convinced that they play both roles to perfection, have either the vocation of a mistress or the vocation of a mother.

If a young wife wants her marriage to continue to develop harmoniously and to last a lifetime, she ought to double her tenderness for her husband at the moment her first baby is born, because what is a question of destiny for her is merely a role that civilization has invented for him, one which, moreover, he fills with a great deal of zeal and felicity, provided that you don't make him disgusted with it at the start.

(See also Fathers)

PATIENCE

Town clerks ought to give each newly-wed couple a treatise on patience along with the marriage licence, for they will need an unlimited supply of it during their married life.

PEACE

Before it is possible to live in peace with others one must be at peace with oneself – a condition that is also called happiness. People at war with humanity are people who have been unable to achieve internal peace. Peacefulness is not one of the characteristics of youth, and contentment often comes only with old age, for when the senses have calmed down tranquillity spreads to other domains as well. However, even if a person is quite peaceful, others who are not may try to destroy this enviable force, and sometimes one is led into an act of cowardice in order to safeguard one's inner harmony. This is not a worthy procedure, for cowardice leads to self-disgust, and you thus run the risk of upsetting your entire equilibrium. Never permit yourself to be annihilated in this way, and do not try to share your husband's every thought either, whether you have been married for a week or for fifty years.

PERHAPS

The word 'perhaps' is the most effective bait with which to lead on an admirer.

PET

Caressing a man and cuddling a child are very feminine pastimes from which you should expect nothing in return apart from the satisfaction they give you. But although a dog never tires of being scratched behind the ears, men eventually become irritated by too much petting, and very often this web of attention woven around them like a cage gives them a feeling of claustrophobia.

My advice is to pet them only occasionally, so that they do not have time to get used to it.

PHILOSOPHY

Men often boast that they are more philosophical than women, whereas they are above all lazier and more egotistical.

To them being philosophical has come to mean being passive, and they mistake simple inertia for profound wisdom.

PILOTS

Life is such that you unhesitatingly place your own in the hands of strangers, whereas you wouldn't lend fifty pounds to a person who didn't offer you every possible guarantee.

We believe, without ever verifying the fact, that a pilot is a superman with nerves of steel, hands of rare precision, and that he is endowed with unerring judgment. From this point it requires only a little more imagination to turn him into a TV or film hero. Alas, a pilot is also a man, and as such he is neither perfect, nor infallible. Thank heavens there are often two of them in an aeroplane!

PIRATES

There are many more of them than is generally believed, and they are by no means all sailing the southern seas. In fact they prefer to gather in large cities where they bask in the general esteem accorded to success and money.

You may very well marry a pirate and never realize it. Modern pirates are simply businessmen who are shrewder and less scrupulous than their colleagues, like the person who is described as 'a hardheaded businessman'.

PITY

Pity is a sentiment that is incompatible with love, for which it is, moreover, merely a pale substitute.

To accord a date, a kiss or one's favours to a man because you pity him is weak and terribly stupid. People who attempt to obtain something by deliberately inspiring this sentiment are simply 'love beggars', who will suffer even more when everybody has become tired of feeling sorry for them.

But the most common form of pity is the pity one feels for oneself, and which ends in tears, in neurasthenia, and, at the extreme limit, in suicide.

PLAYBOY

The playboy is international, he is handsome, he is rich and he is willing to go to any expense in order to obtain publicity. He is ready to marry and divorce as often as necessary in order to obtain an income. He will cross an ocean to attend a party, and he will punch a photographer and smash his camera only if he sure that there is another photographer present to record the scene.

He is a monstrous snob and, like all monsters, he possesses a certain charm. Furthermore, he is endowed with taste and a wide but superficial culture. He is an arbiter of elegance and launches fashions. He is, in short, an ideal public relations director for a luxury industry, but he is the last person in the world with whom a woman should fall in love unless she is a famous heiress.

He does not know how to grow old gracefully, and the kindest fate for him is to die at the height of his glory before he has been forgotten.

POCKETS

If handbags hadn't been invented and if we had to stuff our pockets as men do, it is certain that our clothes would not hang so well. But all the necessary identification cards, driver's licences, credit cards, and chequebooks, not to mention cigarettes and lighters, swim about in men's pockets. The father of a large family who, in addition to his personal documents, carries over his heart the snapshots of his darling wife and all the children sometimes seems to have a deformity. In any case, if the man of your life cannot live without his ball-point pen and if he carries it in his breast pocket, make him change it to an inside pocket for nothing is less elegant than the visible tip of a pen; it's almost as bad as if he stuck it behind his ear.

Shy men seem to fumble in their pockets not only for their cigarettes but also for their courage. Have you ever noticed that as soon as a man senses that people are watching him he sticks his hands in his pockets with the air of a person who wishes to appear relaxed and casual? But it only proves how very ill at ease he is. Two men out of three plunge their hands into their pockets the moment they enter a restaurant and wait for the maître d'hôtel to assign them a table, although they wouldn't dream of doing the same when waiting for the train or bus. Try to rid them of this habit, because it betrays an unfortunate lack of self-assurance.

POETS

A poet is not only a gentleman who writes verses; he is also a man who perceives things that other men never even suspect; he is like a prism that decomposes a ray of sunshine into a rainbow; he is the prisoner who tames a spider; the hunter who, dazzled by the plumage of a bird or the graceful movements of a rabbit, lays down his gun without shooting; he is the racing pilot who slows down in order to admire a cloud; the fashion designer who gives a dress to a penniless pretty girl; the Salvation Army chef who creates a fancy mounted dessert on a weekday; the blind man who sings of the coloured autumn leaves; the pedestrian who, enchanted by the tender green of the first spring leaves, fails to notice a traffic light of the same colour and becomes the butt of the rush-hour drivers' insults; he is the caretaker of a sordid block of flats who lovingly grows geraniums in a dark courtyard.

Being a poet is living twice as intensely as an ordinary man; it's like having four eyes, four ears and four hands, the better to see, hear and feel the wonders nature has created for us. So while I do not advise you to marry a poet whose only job is writing poetry – because my editor will tell you that nowadays poetry is profitable only in the form of song lyrics – you should nevertheless try to select as your life companion a man who will be capable of taking you by the hand to admire the moonlight on the evening of a televised boxing match, or one whose mind is occasionally elevated above the usual masculine preoccupations – ice-cold martinis, rising sales curves, and good golf scores – in order to talk about the *Roman de la Rose* or, more prosaically, about the changing colour of your eyes.

POSSESSIVENESS

Every individual has the right to a little garden in which he can walk alone without being spied on by the neighbours. If the man you love always wants to know what you are thinking about, what you dreamed of, and why you have changed the shade of your stocking, don't smile and think that this is love; he is the most insidious kind of tyrant – a tyrant who wants to know all, to control everything, and to practically breathe for you. Break off these stifling bonds while there is still time, before you have been completely crushed by them.

I wonder if it isn't finally simpler to live with an egotist who leaves you in peace, rather than a person who is so possessive that he wants to know the slightest detail of your every thought.

POUNDS

For many years now it has not been at all elegant for a woman to be plump, but until recently this was not the case with men. They acquired their overweight much later than we, at the same time as they acquired honours, to which it was, you might say, the natural complement; a man had to be stout in order to impress the public.

The youthful modern fashions have revolutionized not only dresses but also masculine figures, for it is quite a trick to squeeze a big stomach into a tight-fitting jacket. And so the unfair discrepancy between their acceptable corpulence and our shameful plumpness is in the process of disappearing, and it is one more victory for women to make men go on diets too.

POWDER

Beware, unfaithful husbands! Powder and lipstick leave eloquent traces on men's jackets, even though disposable Kleenex has replaced the lipstick-smeared handkerchief, source of many a domestic drama!

PROSTATE

The prostate is a feature granted exclusively to men and it therefore assumes enormous importance in their lives. You can still joke about their appendices and even show them your own scar, but the prostate is a gland that belongs to them alone and they are constantly aware of it — even when it is functioning properly. The only suitable tone of voice for mentioning it to them is the hushed, awed and admiring whisper that is generally reserved for visiting cathedrals.

PRUDES

While prudery is outdated in women, it is practically suspect in men, because one wonders what sort of shameful complex is being concealed by a man who refuses to call a spade a spade.

PUBERTY

While growing old is much less difficult for a man than for a woman, puberty is a much more painful period for a boy than for a girl. Added to the complexes created by a changing voice, a face covered with pimples, and the shadow of a moustache, a nose, hands and feet that have grown faster than the rest, an awkward air and a lanky body is the fact that girls of the same age are a thousand times more attractive, more intelligent and already perfectly adapted to the career of seduction that shrewd businessmen and blind parents tend to impose on them at an even earlier age. The poor mother sees her adorable nestling transformed into a graceless duck from one day to the next. Instead of complaining, she should realize that her baby sees the cosy universe of his childhood falling to pieces; he bumps into things wherever he turns; and the more unhappy of the two – even if he is hateful to her – is not the one she thinks.

She might buy a good lotion for his pimples, but she should leave to her husband the responsibility of giving him the advice that will make them disappear for good.

PYJAMAS

Even the most conservative man in the world at the office may dress with a bit more originality in bed. Besides, he should consider the fact that, just as he hates to see his wife in a long flannel nightgown, she may not feel like sleeping next to a convict in stripes.

The most elegant pyjamas are, of course, of silk or sheer cotton in plain bright colours. Many men hate to wear pyjama trousers to bed, but they should always wear them underneath their dressing-gowns because I know of few things as unattractive as hairy male calves emerging from beneath a lovely silk gown.

QUALITY/QUANTITY

Since fashions change every six months, a woman can still claim that she prefers to renew her wardrobe frequently rather than to invest a large sum in one well-tailored suit. But this reasoning is never valid for a man, who can be elegant only when he is dressed in garments of very good quality.

And so, madame, if he consults you on his wardrobe, insist on quality. Cashmere sweaters will last for ten years, if you know how to wash them correctly and to keep the moths away; a camel's-hair coat, a suède jacket, fine-quality golf shoes or patent leather evening pumps, a handsome umbrella (if he isn't absent-minded), cufflinks that seem terribly extravagant – all of these things add up to masculine elegance; but certainly not the latest plaid cotton jacket or the newest fad T-shirt.

QUARRELS

Some couples are so bored together that they feel alive only when they quarrel; it is their last remaining form of communication.

Newlyweds' quarrels are of a different nature, for they are caused by the discovery – not always a happy one – that each makes of the other, and by the painful adjustment of two different characters. In addition to the passionate reconciliation scenes that can follow lovers' quarrels, there may also develop a better mutual comprehension. But young couples would be unwise to underestimate the importance of their first disputes, and especially to become accustomed to this form of expression, because there will come a day – or rather, a night – when, instead of reconciling, they will turn their backs on each other and thus establish a climate of hostility that can breed only divorce.

As for quarrelsome strangers, the only attitude they merit is one of scornful silence.

QUESTIONS

There are certain questions that we regret ever having posed, and with age we realize that certain facts are better left unlearned.

So if you are afraid of knowing exactly what was the role of your cousin from Chester in your husband's life while you were so ill, it would be better not to ask the question: besides, either a husband is civilized and tells a lie, or he is brutal and tells the truth.

The only questions that should never be evaded are the ones that children ask; in fact, you should reply with the greatest sincerity if you do not want them to stop coming to you for advice and information.

RAGE

Certain volatile persons fly into a rage for no reason at all, and you see apparently normal people become livid or crimson on the most futile pretexts. Even if he possesses every possible virtue, a man who is afflicted with this malady (because it is nothing more than an illness) must either be given a tranquillizer after a doctor is consulted, or else be permitted to smash everything in the house while you hide behind a door. In the latter case, it is advisable to buy all your dishes from Woolworths. Furthermore, if he ever brings home a pretty Arab dagger as a paper-knife or a bronze paperweight, hurry up and hide it – even if this makes him fly into a rage!

RAZORS

Think of his razor as a rare museum piece that it is forbidden to touch without special permission.

REGRETS

Sooner or later in life we all have to make a choice between remorse for having done too much and regret for not having done enough. I think there is no doubt that, while women sometimes feel remorse for having been unfaithful to their husbands, the latter regret the women they never had, and the best way to make a man remember you is not to sleep with him.

The most painful regrets are those you feel in realizing that you have let an opportunity escape you through sheer laziness; and the most unbearable remorse results from hurting somebody you love.

But if you do your best day after day, taking advantage of the sunshine and learning to appreciate beauty, and if you have never perpetrated an evil act simply for the pleasure of causing harm, then you can finish your life with neither too many regrets nor too much remorse.

REJUVENATION

If you really want to be rejuvenated, it isn't enough to smear yourself with cream or to have your face lifted; you must also refrain from 'thinking old'.

The two best recipes for rejuvenation are: surrounding oneself with young people and trying to understand them; and falling in love, even late in life.

RELIGION

You should respect his as he should respect yours. A woman changes her religion in order to marry the man she loves more readily than does a man in the same situation – and yet there are more women than men who go to church.

REPAIRS

Females should learn how to make minor household repairs at the same time they learn to spell. I am enraged at my clumsiness whenever I try to drive a nail, and at my inability to do without a man whenever there is the slightest breakdown; and yet I can embark all alone on a trip around the world without a qualm.

REPROACHES

A direct reproach is always negative. If you say to some-body, and especially to a man: 'You were quite wrong to do that, it was completely stupid' – you will be right, but he will hate you. People dislike losing face, and the normal reaction in order to save appearances is to persist in one's mistake. But if you say to him: 'Because of what you thought you had to do, now we will have to try to patch things up in such and such a way', he will be filled with remorse and will do anything to make amends.

The more reproaches you make, the more reasons

you will have for making them. So why not try instead the technique of cheerful punishment? Instead of reproaching your husband for keeping dinner waiting for an hour while he enjoyed himself in a bar with an old buddy, serve him an overcooked meal – with your apologies. Instead of displaying a tear-stained face when you learn that he was seen in a night-club with a beautiful blonde, go to the cinema and try to come home five minutes later than he does, even if you have to sit through the film three times and then hide behind a tree until he returns. And above all, don't immediately tell him where you were. He will surely be very uneasy.

Instead of spending two hours a day tidying your son's room, screaming with rage, leave it as it is. Perhaps he will soon get tired of living in the debris of an earthquake. And if he ruins his clothes out of pure negligence, well, let him wear ruined clothes. He will begin to be more careful the day his little girl-friend tells him he is dirty.

One is always punished for all the mistakes one makes, so there is no point in going to the bother of acting like a commanding officer. Reproaches do not serve the slightest purpose – except to make you unpopular.

RESTAURANTS

Study men carefully in restaurants, for in these places their characters show up and you can see at once whether a man is timid or sure of himself, generous or stingy, a glutton or a gourmet, attentive or egotistical, witty or boring – in other words, whether or not it would be worth your while to become interested in him.

SALARIES

It is obviously much more comfortable to live on two salaries rather than one, but it is still preferable for the husband's to be the larger of the two. It now happens more and more frequently that a woman holds a more important job than does her husband, and the husband can resent the situation. She ought to ask him for advice as often as possible, even if she doesn't intend to follow it; she should let him choose the new car, and she should encourage him to buy clothes as costly as her own.

In short, she should be sufficiently modest for him still to have the impression that he is protecting her. (See also Money)

SCENT

While our grandfathers were permitted at the very most to smell faintly of lavender, tobacco and Russian leather in order to be attractive to our grandmothers, their grandsons now have at their disposition at least ten first-class brands of toiletries that propose to improve on their natural odour with scented soap, talcum powder, eau-de-Cologne, after-shave lotion, etc., and you now hear men discussing the comparative merits of Aramis or Gucci as ardently as their wives. The names of the products made especially for them have been carefully selected to avoid the slightest suggestion of effeminacy, and it is rather surprising that none of them has yet been christened Lion Tamer or Commando. The important manufacturers are feverishly preparing creams and make-up bases for men, and we are joyfully entering the era of the male peacock; barracks effluvia have become ancient history. If you wish to please them, mesdames, when you kiss them in public – don't fail to gush: 'Really divine, my dear!' It can also spare you the trouble of hunting for unusual Christmas gifts.

SEX

I sincerely believe that by abandoning all their former modesty women are preparing a disillusioned future for themselves.

By telling women that they can feel the same pleasure as men and that they have the same right to it, certain shrewd 'doctors' have undoubtedly made fortunes, but they have done their patients no real service. Besides, they haven't invented anything new, anything not covered by the *Kama Sutra*, the erotic engravings of ancient Greece to those of eighteenth-century France, of the Chinese and Japanese prints, etc., which amply illustrated the thirty-two positions. At the risk of being considered irretrievably old-fashioned, I cannot conceive of love as a form of Swedish gymnastics or a cooking recipe to be followed faithfully from a book.

The very basis of feminine seduction is mystery, and the shy virgin in a long-sleeved night-dress of the Victorian era seems to be more seductive to a man than the dishevelled mare who insists on so many orgasms per hour because she has read that she has a right to them.

There is not a single example of Don Juanism bringing happiness to men or, with even more reason, to women. If men are becoming more and more disinterested in women – and the increasing number of homosexuals is proof of it – it is because women openly display all their charms and because there is nothing left for men to teach them.

Finally, it is unimaginable that centuries of poetry should be erased by this clinical conception of love, and that a good lover should no longer be anything more than a specialist who has made a study of the correct reflexes, exactly like the doctor who knows where to hit with his little hammer in order to make your leg rise.

If Frenchmen enjoy a flattering reputation as lovers throughout the world, I do not think it is because they have greater endurance in bed than other men, but because they have always known how to surround the act itself, which is the same for all mammals, with embellishments of wit, imagination and tender phrases, all of which are far more effective than mere technique. It is a well-known fact, moreover, that streetwalkers, who are crammed with technique – and for good reason – are almost always frigid.

So instead of rushing to buy all those handbooks that can only result in disappointment, women would do better to content themselves with the men whom they have chosen – wisely, I hope – and to make them happier by letting them discover little by little all that they are capable of giving them.

SHARING

Let's be objective. We share our husbands' destinies much more than they share ours. If a woman marries an idiot she vegetates throughout her life, whereas if a man marries an idiot the consequences are less serious; he simply takes his friends out to dinner instead. But a woman usually adopts her husband's name, his habits and the domicile that he has chosen.

Every young girl ought to consider this before marrying the first handsome lad who asks her; but she always thinks she knows better than her parents, who have learned from experience that pretty faces don't get any prettier as time goes by and that love and fantasy are soon drowned in the kitchen sink and the washing-machine.

SHAVING

Shaving is a ritual that holds an important place in a man's life. The first rendezvous a lad keeps with his razor and mirror is the first session of self-communion that will afterwards be repeated every morning of his life. Even the least fastidious men shave with a certain amount of ceremony and personal idiosyncrasy. Don't think for a moment that you will ever succeed in changing their ways, but on the contrary see to it that they always have everything they need at their fingertips; after-shave lotion or shaving cream, a certain mirror or a special kind of razor blade – and then tiptoe out of the bathroom, for this is the moment when a vain man worships his reflection in the mirror, when an optimist sings cheerfully of glorious tomorrows, and when a pessimist thinks that he certainly looks like H— and that life really isn't worth the bother of . . . shaving.

SHIRTS

Even men who aren't the least bit fastidious about their clothes become very fussy where their shirts are concerned.

While it would be an exaggeration to claim that a shirt makes the man, it is nevertheless true that wearing a shirt elevates the savage to the rank of a civilized citizen. Closer to home, the fact that men in turtle-neck sweaters are not admitted to smart restaurants might be interpreted as an indication that a shirt is a symbol of integration in modern society. As for dictators, one of the first things they do in order to distinguish their followers from the crowd is to dress them up in black or red shirts according to their moods.

I goes without saying that in order for a shirt to be elegant, no matter what its shape or colour, it must be absolutely spotless, and in the polluted air of our modern cities a man must change his shirt every day. It must also fit well, with sleeves neither too short nor too long, and a collar neither too wide nor too tight. It should never blouse above the belt, but fit the shape of the torso.

SHOPPING

Men generally do not like to shop in large department stores, and while you see their busily efficient wives gracefully wending their way through the milling crowds with the determined air of swallows returning to their village in the spring, the husbands are so afraid of losing them that they never take their eyes off them, not even in order to look at the merchandise on display. Men prefer small shops where they are waited on and where a salesgirl will advise them. They are so unaccustomed to shopping alone that some of them even ask their wives to buy their underwear and ties, or take their wives with them the day they decide to buy a complete new wardrobe – which is usually the day when everything they own is falling apart at the seams.

Men provide the most comical spectacle in grocer's shops; they may assume the relaxed air of connoisseurs, but they haven't the faintest notion.

SHORTS

Every man reaches an age when it is preferable for him to wear long trousers, even if he looks like a retired colonel in the British Indian Army.

In any case, shorts are appropriate only on the beach, in a boat or on a tennis court, and they can be worn only with sandals, tennis shoes or espadrilles. A combination of knee-length khaki shorts, high wool socks and heavy leather shoes is the uniform of the Boy Scouts, and it should be exclusively reserved for them.

SILENCE

Nine times out of ten we regret having spoken, and without acting like underwater skin-divers all our lives, we should nevertheless remain silent a little oftener.

Between lovers, more misunderstandings arise from ill-chosen words than from caresses.

As for employers, everybody knows that you must listen to them religiously if you want them to think you are intelligent.

Silence also implies discretion, and if you are curious but noted for your ability to keep a secret, you will learn a lot more than if you are talkative.

SINS

Men generally take pride in making us commit some of the seven capital sins, with lust at the head of the list, followed by gluttony. They claim that we are more slothful and more envious than they are, but they admit to being more prideful, more avaricious, and especially more prone to anger.

It is difficult to establish a list of preferences, since all these sins should horrify us equally; but it seems to me that avarice, synonym of unconcern for one's neighbours, causes the most harm to others, whereas the six remaining sins destroy only the unhappy person who indulges in them.

SKIN

A nice complexion is almost as important to a man as to a woman, and men are beginning to realize it. If I were a manufacturer of bathroom furniture, I should start making medicine cabinets twice as large as in the past, because men will soon be using as many beauty products as women do.

SLAPS

It is always a shock to get one's face slapped, even for a very westernized man, and this rather expedious procedure should be resorted to only in case of grave offence. If an obviously drunken gentleman insists on kissing you, you can give him a sharp slap; and you can give the same treatment to the man who mistakes your panties for a sort of amulet that must be touched in order to bring good luck. But do not seize the slightest pretext to slap people whose humour escapes you or even those who say disobliging things to you; if you are not gifted at repartee, your best response is simply cold disdain.

I almost forgot – if your husband ever slaps you, telephone your lawyer at once – unless you yourself are guilty of terrible deeds and deserve a hundred slaps along with a spanking; in that case, and in that case only, you should generously forgive him – and secretly rejoice, for now that he has put himself in the wrong you can serenely forget your own crimes.

SLIPPERS

Show me your bedroom slippers and I will tell you how old you are.

You start out in life with tiny sky-blue booties knitted by your mother. You start marriage barefoot; but you soon start to sit down to breakfast in slippers.

Finally, the day when your grandchildren bring you a pair of fur-lined slippers, you may as well admit that you have grown old.

SMILES

Everyone knows that they ought to smile, but how many people smile with their eyes as well? As a matter of fact, if you cannot see an accompanying spark of sympathy or humour in the eyes, a smile is nothing but a mechanical facial movement or one more modern grimace. Important men do not smile very often, unless they are in politics, where it is obligatory to beam with radiant demagogic and electoral warmth.

I know of nothing more painful than to see a broadly smiling employee who does not receive a smile in return. Smiles should be like handshakes, and since etiquette decrees that it is up to the boss, the customer or the woman to be the first to hold out her hand, it is also up to them to be the first to smile.

SMOKING

Smoking is the most widespread vice in the world as well as the one that is most stupidly tolerated and even encouraged. Nevertheless, while suggesting a lack of self-control similar to the weak will of a drunkard, it must be admitted that the harmful effects of tobacco become apparent much later than the effects of drink. Still, an inveterate smoker is not exactly the Prince Charming you dreamed of at the age of ten.

A habitual smoker strews ashes all over the carpets and rubs them in with the tip of his shoe; he burns holes in all his clothes; if he smokes in bed he endangers the lives of the entire household; he coughs and spits; his teeth are yellow, his breath is bad . . . and he spends a lot of money.

If he smokes cigars, he burns less things but smells even worse and spends more money.

Incidentally, is smoking really the only remedy our modern world has discovered for calming the nerves of its citizens?

SNOBS

The snob is so devoured by his primary passion that there is little room left for other sentiments. While a snob cannot be at the same time a Don Juan, he has much in common with Narcissus, a Narcissus who studies particularly the reflections of the persons he wishes to imitate. He is far from being an ideal lover. He is much too preoccupied with the impression he wants to give to the 'right people'.

In order to have a chance of attracting a snob, a woman must possess a great name or at least a great fortune, beauty perhaps, and certainly chic. When you have won the snob of your dreams and when you have become Mrs Snob, there remains the problem of living with him. So say goodbye at once to your nice school chum, to the cottage in the country, to dinners in good but unfashionable restaurants, to non-pedigreed dogs, to the Ford that ran so well, to the television serial you used to enjoy so much, to the *Reader's Digest*, to the Costa Brava where you spent such marvellous holidays – goodbye, in fact, to the slightest expression of a personality that does not conform to that of your husband's clan.

Nobody is more conformist than a snob.

SNORING

If he really snores like a vacuum cleaner, don't get angry or play the role of an insomniac martyr; simply go and sleep on the sofa in the living-room.

SOCIETY

If there is one thing that we have the power to control, it is the company we keep.

When you marry, you also wed the society in which your husband lives, and I'd be willing to bet that the young theatre usherette who recently married a millionaire no longer sees her old girl-friends very often.

Climbing to the top of the social ladder requires money first of all, but you also have to enjoy the game, which demands a great deal of time and energy. In the long run, the best means of frequenting intelligent or amusing people is to be intelligent or amusing oneself. Thus, by marrying an imbecile, even a very rich one, you are condemning yourself to a life surrounded by bores.

SOCKS

An article of clothing as banal as socks can completely demolish an impeccable outfit. The moment a man sits down, his socks are one of the first things you notice, and men who wear socks that bare their calves should be relegated, in my opinion, to the caste of untouchables. Other errors: tired socks that fall limply around the ankles; certain novelty patterns, and certain horizontal stripes that look like a jail uniform.

For sportswear, it is more chic to wear lighter socks rather than beige or grey ones. But whenever you wear a business suit, the socks should be dark, they should reach high enough never to reveal flesh, stay up and they should be of fine wool.

SONS

A word as sweet as honey in the mouth of every woman, it encompasses the purest love, the most overwhelming affection, the blindest indulgence, the greatest pride, the most complete success, but also the most unbearable anguish and the most incurable despair. All these maternal emotions are so exclusive and so violent that a mother is not always an ideal educator, and in the absence of a father it is very difficult for her to keep her floods of tenderness under control behind the dam of firmness that is absolutely necessary to a child's education. Nothing is more difficult than to evaluate with total objectivity the qualities of one's children, and particularly of one's son, for the mother-son relationship is absolutely exceptional, beginning nine months before birth and ending only at death, with the eternal admiration women feel toward men as a supplementary attraction, and we should therefore be forgiving with unduly doting mothers.

As everyone knows, the more terrible of the two mothers-in-law is the mother of the bridegroom, and this is quite understandable. After observing, with an air of amusement and complicity, her son flit from flirtations to love affairs, she feels her power begin to crumble as soon as he really falls in love, and it requires great self-control for her merely to be pleasant with her daughter-in-law. She feels toward her a very complex sentiment consisting of the desire to dominate – therefore wishing her to be as malleable and as colourless as possible – and at the same time the disappointment in seeing her handsome, intelligent son marry such an insignificant creature. If, on the contrary, her daughter-in-law is more brilliant or richer than her son, she develops a violent jealousy – mixed with a certain admiration. In any case, she realizes that her reign is brought to an end with the fateful words: 'I do.' I know certain women who have lived only for their sons and who, after their sons' marriage, became if not disinterested at least detached from them, and lost no time in running to hold the hands of their husbands, whom they had rather neglected during the previous twenty-five years. If the young couple's life should not go smoothly, and even if it is the husband who behaves like a cad, his mother nevertheless considers deep down in her heart that he must be in the right.

There have been so many vulgar jokes on the subject of mothers-in-law that these maligned women generally make a superhuman effort to win their daughter-in-laws' affections, and if you are seeking proof of civilized behaviour in modern society, this is certainly a striking example! But peaceful coexistence between these two women is always somewhat precarious and depends above all on the young husband, who should be adult enough to get along without his mother and at the same time to maintain toward her an affection that is at last devoid of ulterior motives.

If the law of nature – so well accepted by animals and so badly by humans – which decrees that children should escape from home as soon as their parents have given them the means to do so, were not considered to be ingratitude but a necessary evil; if mothers, having given everything to their sons, did not expect to receive in return eternal gratitude; if, instead of retaining them in the nest as long as possible, they pushed them out of it so that they would fly sooner on their own wings, relations between the two generations would be far more harmonious than they are. But no. The feeling of possessiveness toward a being one has oneself created is too strong. A son has an emotional hold over a woman that all the logic in the world cannot explain away.

However, if you are frank with yourself, you will perceive that you have nothing in common with the younger generation, neither the same preoccupations, the same pastimes, the same language, nor the same tastes. Instead of complaining when, one fine day, at about the age of thirteen, your plump, cute baby boy is suddenly transformed into a weird bean-pole and becomes uncommunicative, stubborn and evasive, you should take consolation in the fact that everything will work itself out in about ten years, and you should try to endure as cheerfully as possible this horrible moment when childhood and its marvellous games are no longer thrilling, when the wounded bird he has tamed, the grasshopper he has imprisoned in a match-box or the guinea-pig in a smelly old shoe-box have not yet been replaced by girls, guitars and motorcycles. It is no fun for parents, but it is even more painful for the child, whose world is falling apart on all sides. This is the period when he goes to war against everything he had theretofore accepted. He suddenly notices that his father has a paunch and looks ridiculous in shorts, that his mother is frightful in hair curlers, that his grandparents know less than he does about the ancient Greeks, that the house is too luxurious or too modest, the car too black, too red, too new, too old. Anything and everything wounds him, he stubs his toes everywhere, and since his unruly appearance is not designed to reassure him, he hates himself as well.

To get along with these hypersensitive creatures

requires exceptional patience and an understanding drawn from the well of one's own childhood memories. You must remember that lectures do no good at all, and that high-sounding words employed right and left at this stage will be emptied of all significance forever after. You must be affectionate and you must be firm. You must be present if, miraculously, one of your children comes to you to unburden a heavy heart. But you must in no case let them walk all over you for fear of giving them complexes if you don't.

Supervised freedom – that is what these unhappy monsters need. But you must remain on guard and observe them through a long-distance telescope, as one observes wild beasts at liberty and enemy armies. You can respect their so-called originality, as long as it doesn't bother you, but there is no reason to suffer from it; they will not be the least bit grateful, but will more likely scorn you for being so weak. You have a right to insist on correct grooming, to make them get their hair cut when it starts to sweep their shoulders and to wash behind their ears, but it would be wrong to break the record that has been playing for the past three hours, unless it is in the living-room. You can forbid their frequenting an undesirable crowd, but it would be sui-cide to read their letters or their diaries.

Finally, a compliment can accomplish far more than a thousand reproaches, for the maladies from which they suffer most acutely are a lack of self-confidence and the anguish of not yet having found their true personalities.

The only help they expect from us is to guide them through the labyrinth of right and wrong, and a woman who has known how to inculcate in her son, by her own example, one or two moral values and a code of life has earned the right to regard with satisfaction in the mirror the wrinkles that the job of being a mother cannot have failed to etch upon her face. They are the most beautiful kind.

STOMACH

Beware of men with stomach trouble; they are sometimes nervous wrecks and always irritable.

STRANGERS

A stranger loses half his charm the day he is no longer a stranger.

STRENGTH

A man may be Hercules on the outside and have the soul of a mouse, or he may be Mickey Mouse with the soul of Hercules. If you ever have to choose between these two types of men, do not hesitate to pick the mouse with the courageous heart.
(See also Courage)

STYLE

Like furniture, human beings have a style. Of course I don't mean to imply that you might have Louis XV legs or a Hepplewhite back, but that your physical appearance, your manner of dress, your choice of pastimes, your job, your home, your marriage, all have a certain style that reflects your personality as an individual or as a married couple.

A woman always has an interest in determining the kind of image she wants to present to the world and then trying to adapt it to her physical appearance and to her means. If you have married a frail and skinny little man, try to give yourself an intellectual style rather than a sporting one, and on Sundays attend a concert instead of a ball game. On the other hand, since nobody has ever died from being other than what he seemed, your skinny little husband may make a crack jockey and you might have great success with a 'racecourse' style. But if you live modestly, don't try to imitate Versailles; rather, adopt a rustic mood and have your curtains made of burlap instead of damask.

The most unattractive quality of an object or of a person is to have no style at all.

SUITORS

Suitors come in all shapes, sizes and ages, but they always have one thing in common: they are either sincere or insincere, and in the latter case I suggest that you refer to the section on 'Don Juans'. The category of sincere suitors is subdivided into two others: those who possess technique and whose who don't.

Suitors who possess technique will lose no time in spotting your weaknesses and determining the best point of attack. This self-assurance is apt to cause their downfall with intelligent women, who are less easily caught in familiar, timeworn traps than are their hare-brained sisters. These traps consist of dancing, presents, compliments ('You're the only woman who, etc.'), sentimental blackmail ('I'd rather die or leave the country . . .'), spicy dishes, strong drink, erotic entertainment, romantic atmosphere (candles, etc.), and also that old line, 'If you refuse to, it's because you don't enjoy it . . .'

Suitors who have no technique are finally more dangerous, because they are so touching. Beware of the maternal instincts that a shy and awkward young man will not fail to arouse in you. If you take him in your arms to console him for his great sorrow, he may very quickly forget that only fifteen minutes earlier he was kneeling in adoration at the feet of an inaccessible goddess and progress to another, less platonic form of activity.

(See also Beau, Boy-friends, Fiancé, Lovers)

SULKINESS

Rancour is such a widespread sentiment that even dogs show it by sulking. My cocker used to hide under a piece of furniture all day long if I went out without him or if I had punished him for some naughtiness. Without wishing to make a comparison, even a flattering one, between the intelligence of my cocker and that of my fellow women, we must admit in all objectivity that we tend to sulk more than men and that it is a horrid fault. I have questioned a number of men concerning the effect of our sulky faces when they have refused us something or when they have offended us, and you would be surprised, my dears, but it is not at all what you have hoped for. They haven't the slightest desire to throw themselves on their knees and beg for forgiveness. On the contrary, they say to themselves: 'Let her pull a long face if she feels like it – as for me, I'm going to the films.' They no longer remember the cause of your sulking, and consequently their sins; they only see the results, which they hate.

Moreover, if you sulk for a long time, you yourself will have forgotten the cause of your bad humour and you will end by creating a permanently unpleasant atmosphere.

No, I really don't believe that we can bring a man to terms by sulking.

SURPRISES

A pleasant surprise can make your heart beat faster, bring colour to your cheeks, and give you the impression of living life instead of moving through it like a sleepwalker. At home, surprises should be used as a therapy for boredom. Instead of always serving the same dishes, invent new ones; change your hair style; refrain from telling everybody what you are going to give them for Christmas; secretly invite your young daughter's friends to a surprise party; decide to go out dancing on the spur of the moment; enter contests and await the results with bated breath; write short stories and submit them to a magazine; in short, borrow the technique of mystery story writers and inject a little suspense into your life. If you plan surprises for yourself and for others, everyone will be caught up in your enthusiasm and perhaps they will start preparing pleasant surprises for you too.

SURRENDER

Never forget that the day you surrender to a man is the day of your defeat and of his victory; the suspense is over and satiety lies ahead.

SWEAT

A man working by the sweat of his brow is perhaps a rather pompous subject for a painting in a Moscow art gallery, but it is a noble subject just the same.

A man who doesn't use deodorants is just as blameworthy as a woman should be; but if he has some on his bathroom shelf, it is up to the woman in his life to see that he uses them!

SWEETHEART

This quite old-fashioned word used to designate a suitor on the point of having his dearest hopes fulfilled; it may still be an official boy-friend, an eternal fiancé, a way of referring to a lover. At school it is a boy who enjoys a special status, a sort of right over you; you go out mostly with him, he gives you a sentimental token of attachment, such as a ring. Either the summer holiday will put an end to your relationship, or you will end up by marrying your sweetheart.

(See also Beau, Fiancé, Lovers, Suitors)

TAMING

A happy marriage is the result of mutual training, but this training can only be accomplished by gentleness and persuasion. Just as a supposedly tamed tiger may one day rebel at the whip and gobble up his trainer, a mousy, submissive woman can run away some fine morning, fed up by the bad treatment inflicted on her by her husband. But when the work of taming has been well done, the beautiful tigress will love her tamer as much as he loves her, and some women who seem ferocious and unapproachable have simply not yet found men who are capable of taming them.

Women have a definite talent for taming, but their technique is not at all the same as that of men; as in all other fields, they rely more on their charm and their disarming sweetness, even on their tears, than on the whip.

TEARS

Some women shed tears as readily as a baby, and it is very irritating. You know that they will turn into fountains at the slightest criticism, and instead of exciting pity, these poor creatures release all the evil sentiments that everybody harbours in the depths of his heart; even the gentlest of persons always conceals a little Marquis de Sade, and his thirst cannot be quenched by tears.

Furthermore, mesdames, if you will think for a minute of the effect men's tears have on you, you will see that things are valued according to their rarity. If, in spite of this good advice, you still feel like indulging in a good cry, at least remove your mascara first – unless you think that by making yourself ugly in the most grotesque fashion you will be even more pitiable.

However, if you know how to weep gracefully or to shed a few pretty crocodile tears at proper moments, you possess a useful art that will make people think of you as a very sensitive kind of woman.

TELEPHONE

Let's be honest about our faults and admit that we enjoy chatting over the telephone. Some women know how to carry on telephone conversations in the curt, businesslike manner of an efficient executive, but most of them have a very characteristic way of ending their sentences with commas instead of periods, which leaves their listeners expecting a long string of words to follow. It is time, mesdames, at your present mental age, to correct this fault, which is sometimes terribly irritating.

TELEVISION

If I have one piece of good advice to give to engaged couples it is to spend several evenings watching television in order to see if their tastes agree. When the period of kisses has passed, this is the principal pastime that remains, and if one of them hates the programmes that the other adores – I wouldn't give very much for their future evenings, or even for the longevity of their marriage.

TEMPERAMENT

It is very easy to blame scenes of uncontrolled anger on a sanguine temperament, incurable laziness on a lymphatic temperament, and nymphomaniac behaviour on one's sex glands. Of course if the 'temperament' is really a psychotic condition, a person does have a few excuses; but normal people should possess sufficient control over their natural tendencies not to let themselves go to extremes.

If you meet a man who continually claims that he 'just happens to be made that way', that his character is the way it is and he can't do anything about it, and if this kind of character doesn't appeal to you or even seem dangerous, do not insist; instead, choose a man who has known how to combat his natural laziness by working even harder than another, or against his biliousness by being friendlier and more cheerful than people who have never had trouble with their lives.

TENDERNESS

The tenderness one feels for another person is a marvellous sentiment that warms the soul. It is very close to love, but much less demanding and more understanding; in fact it is often the final stage of a great passion, and it is more comforting in old age than anything else I know.

Perhaps there is nothing in the world more touching than the sight of a very tender elderly couple.

TIME

Men claim that we are never on time. Personally, I have spent at least fifteen hundred hours waiting for my husband, which amounts to two full months over a period of thirty-one years, and I hate to be kept waiting!

People who are chronically late are badly organized or a little unbalanced; they suffer from the malady of being unable to decide to leave in time. Life is hell with a person who is always late, and I advise you to cure those dear and close to you of this fault by setting a limit to your patience: ten to twenty minutes, after which you will either have left or started your meal without them.

TRAPPING

Neither man nor beast enjoys feeling that a trap is about to close upon him, and as soon as he senses its presence, his reaction is to flee. So if you have decided to set a trap for a young man, the last thing you should do is to let him become aware of your intentions.

The education of young girls has always centred around the art of 'how to catch a husband', and the education of boys has centred around the necessity of 'how to avoid feminine traps'. Formerly the essential asset of a young girl was her virginity, together with her dowry; now this is largely a thing of the past.

In the upper classes, decades ago, husband-hunting was practised only in drawing-rooms by the parents themselves, and there was no opportunity for a well-bred young girl to meet men elsewhere than at chaperoned dances – which is one reason why a misalliance was so much more scandalous. But now the hunting grounds have moved from drawing-rooms to universities and, if a husband hasn't turned up there, to offices. In the Paris Medical School alone, ten per cent of the women students admit having enrolled only in order to meet a future doctor, and the supreme triumph for a girl is to capture him when he is in his last year and she is only in her first.

Men students to whom I have spoken were very sensitive on this subject, and if twenty per cent of them marry while they are still at university they know very well that they are choice quarry for the girls who, once they have graduated, will never again find such a marvellous game preserve. And so they are very quick to sense the approach of a magazine-style 'siren', with all her arsenal of artificial seduction, her assets in full display, and her well-learned lessons. It would seem that only idiots are now foolish enough to let themselves be caught by such means. The rest of the young men quickly drop girls who are:

– over-possessive and who make a scene if, after three consecutive Saturday night dates at the films they take another girl to the football match;

– too aggressive as to the future; they detest being quizzed about their future plans, the number of children they'd like to have, and their favourite colour in bedspreads;

– too eager to have them meet the girl's parents

– and, in general, all girls who overdo things.

I was surprised and delighted to note that, in the final analysis, young men still appreciate the same qualities in a woman and that at the top of the list they still put 'sweetness', 'discretion', and 'understanding'. They still ask for nothing more than to protect their wives, to offer them their names and to support them, but they don't want to be treated like insects that are slowly devoured by the females they have fertilized. They are willing to make all the important decisions together, and they have admitted that their wives have the same right to sexual pleasure as they do, but they still wish to retain the illusion that they are the ones who dispense it. After centuries of being the masters, they don't want to be reduced all of a sudden to the rank of mere tools or women's slaves.

And so my advice, dear huntress Diana, is to conceal your bow and arrows, to banish the word 'marriage' from your conversation as well as the motto, so dear to the French, of 'Liberty, Equality, Fraternity', to seek advice rather than to give it, to radiate human warmth and bourgeois comfort – in order to let yourself finally be 'caught' by the man of *your* choice.

TRAVEL

I often wonder why some women insist on travelling, because from the moment they leave home you hear them complain about everything: it's too cold, it's too hot, they're seated over the train's wheels or the plane's wing, the mattress is too hard or too soft, there's no hot water in the bathroom, there are mosquitoes in the bedroom or flamenco singers under the window – in short they turn the trip (and their husband's too) into a veritable cross-bearing procession.

Men generally complain much less, but it is still a good test to take a trip with one's fiancé. If he smooths over every problem, moves ahead of you to open doors and doesn't let you carry anything, if he reserves the best table in the dining-car and orders in advance a chilled bottle of champagne, if he cheerfully repairs a flat tyre and is willing to leave the motorway to have tea on a lovely riverbank, if he thinks of everything in advance, if he is imperturbable even when one of the plane's motors bursts into flames, and if you feel that nothing can harm you as long as you are at his side – marry him as soon as possible!

If, on the other hand, he complains about the porters, is stingy with his tips, doesn't succeed in getting good service, grumbles all the time, has sore feet, drinks nothing but mineral water, rushes into planes in order to grab a seat next to the emergency exit, thinks only of the number of miles per hour he's going to average between Paris and Deauville – run away as fast as you can, for he is a miser and an egoist, and to top it all he is narrow-minded. No lecture course in marriage could ever equal a brief premarital trip as an obligatory prerequisite to a marriage licence.

TRICKS

You certainly have more than one trick in your bag, but, as with your menus, be sure to vary them as soon as they start to lose their novelty.

TWO

Two people in bed, in a restaurant, on holiday, and in life in general, is the ideal number, and I have never understood why young people want to multiply it so quickly. They would do better to exhaust all the selfish pleasures for two before becoming involved in the adventure of raising a big family.

U

UNDRESSING

It is now often sufficient to unzip a zipper in order to entirely undress a woman. Our grandfathers must have had the impression of gaining a hard-won victory when they came to our grandmothers' last petticoat, but their grandchildren can achieve the same results in the time it takes to say 'Zip . . . and whoosh!' A strip-tease is now, you might say, a museum that perpetuates a long-forgotten tradition.

But masculine undressing has apparently never been considered an art, for to my knowledge there is no such thing as masculine strip-tease, except as a form of slapstick comedy.

UNEMPLOYED

Being the wife of a man who is out of work is not very easy, for not only has she less money to keep the pot boiling, but she also must bolster the morale of her husband, who is unhappy about losing his job and thus giving the impression that he is either incompetent or unlucky. He feels that he is in the way at home, that he is an object of vaguely scornful pity on the part of the neighbours, and he doesn't know what to do with the free time that he used to long for when he was working.

The first thing to do, therefore, is to keep him busy during the time that is not occupied in seeking another job – and to keep him busy without its costing you too much. According to his talents, you can have him repaint the kitchen or the garden furniture, patch up the pram or repair an old radio. But, most of all, you must never show the anguish you feel about the future. You should, on the contrary, tell him that you have complete confidence in him, that with his ability he will find a much more interesting job than the one he lost, and that you have a little nest egg which will help to see you through this difficult period. If his morale is high he will find a job much more easily than if he has a defeated air. All this is very easy to write, but it is not at all easy to put into practice, for a discouraged man may start to drink, to be unjust, bitter and even nasty; and one more good reason for a wife to have a career of her own is that she will never be completely at the mercy of such a catastrophe.

UNPOLISHED

Even diamonds need to be polished, and good manners have never harmed a soul. If you are sufficiently enamoured of a woodsman who behaves like a grizzly bear to train him in the basic social graces, bravo! You must possess all the patience and talent required for teaching, and it would be a pity to waste them. Personally, I haven't the patience; and besides, I would rather have a well-polished gem than a diamond in the rough.

UPBRINGING

A man can learn from a good book how to dress and how to entertain, but he can develop a certain refinement of the heart only if he has seen an example of it in his youth, for our childhood experiences condition all the rest of our lives.

VANITY

All men, even those who seem most modest, indulge in some form of vanity. One man is proud of his amorous prowess, another of his swimming crawl, a third of the top speed of his car. It is sufficient to discover the object of a person's vanity and then to flatter him about it in order to make a friend of him. 'I've been told you have the most beautiful roses in England' to a gardening maniac or 'Rumour has it that you dance like a dream!' to an old-fashioned one-step expert, will attract the homage of these gentlemen even more surely than if you were Brigitte Bardot. But beware of too obvious charms and over-vaunted merits; for example, Michèle Morgan, whose eyes won the admiration of the entire world, preferred the line of her nose. It is therefore preferable to praise a very handsome man for his wit and a genius for his beautiful eyes.

VENICE

Visiting Venice at the age of twenty with the man you love is certainly a marvellous experience, but it is even more marvellous to have Venice in your heart and to be abler to share romantic sighs in front of Victoria Station.

I know, alas, a lot of people think that Venice smells bad . . .

VIRGINITY

Fifty years ago, losing her virginity was a very serious decision for a young girl to make, as well as a degradation in the eyes of her family and of society; but in this day and age it seems old-fashioned to preserve it. We have gone from one extreme to the other.

But, mesdemoiselles, although you needn't attach the same importance to virginity as in former times, it would be foolish to lose it carelessly in the back seat of a car at the first opportunity, for tomorrow you may meet the man of your life and you will regret not having waited for him.

VIRILITY

There is often a tendency to confuse virility with brutality, and to think that a man who knows how to be tender or refined is not entirely virile. True virility is much more a question of emotional reactions than of physical prowess. I can remember seeing a boxing champion gesticulate in front of the television camera in a manner that suggested a hysterical woman much more than a man possessing all the qualities generally attributed to virility. Killers and gangsters are much less virile to my mind than an honest employee who is never involved in any adventure and who goes to his office every morning in some government building, post office or bank, but who gives his family the security, warmth and tenderness of a home.

VOICES

A man's voice, like his hands, is extremely important, for he can no more disguise one than he can the other. Merely by hearing a man speak, even without seeing him, you can tell whether he is distinguished, violent, nervous or shy, if he is in a good mood or furiously angry – and in the last two instances his dog is just as perceptive as you are.

The seductive power of a beautiful voice is fantastic, and tenors or crooners always have a flock of admirers trailing behind them. Personally, the voices of Sir Laurence Olivier and the old BBC announcers always filled me with bliss, and as for General de Gaulle, it was certainly not his physical appearance that attracted the women's votes that contributed so much to his political success.

WEDDINGS

When a wedding is an intimate informal ceremony and the bride does not wear the traditional long white wedding-gown, it is sufficient for the groom to wear a dark suit, white shirt, plain tie and black shoes. But things become more complicated when the fiancée insists on having her day of glory and is determined to respect every detail of the well-established formal wedding ritual.

All the men in the family should then wear morning coats, and most men prefer to hire rather than to buy them.

The groom arrives discreetly before the triumphant bride makes her appearance and he thus assumes for the first time the role of a man waiting for his wife, without realizing that most often this is merely the beginning of a long series of such scenes. In general the poor man doesn't feel at all like laughing even if he is madly in love, but he can console himself by thinking that the ceremony doesn't last very long and that his best man will have thought of everything – including the ring. This is, incidentally, a very important role, which it is inadvisable to assign to a scatterbrain, because a best man should be able to act as nursemaid, and even as nurse if the libations of the night before have left their mark, as valet (preparing the clothes and luggage), travel agent (reserving the rooms, the plane tickets, filling the car with petrol), master of ceremonies (manoeuvring the bridesmaids and the elderly invalid aunt, proposing the first toast to the newlyweds while quieting the crowd of guests) and sometimes also as a morale booster.

It is a glorious and exhausting day, and everyone will want to have a photograph. In order not inspire the hilarity of three generations, I advise the groom to pay attention to where he places his hands and gloves, and to try to seem less ecstatic and at the same time as natural as possible.

When the moment arrives for him to go away with his bride, he changes into an elegant travelling ensemble – there will be plenty of time later on to dress in his old blue jeans and sweater.

WIDOWERS

These rare birds are even more interesting than bachelors, because at least you can be sure a widower isn't a woman-hater – or, if he has become one, it's because he was unhappily married, and now that he is finally free again he ought to feel very cheerful. However, some widowers do indeed seem inconsolable, or perhaps they don't wish to be consoled – I have never quite been able to tell the difference with the few examples I have met. A widower who is still spry and sufficiently rich is so choice a prey for certain lonely, ageing women that it's easy to see why he locks himself up in a fortress of eternal mourning, which has the advantage of attracting sympathy and attention, and at the same time protecting him from a new marriage in which he hasn't the slightest desire to get involved.

If you ever have the opportunity to console a widower, you must be prepared to withstand a comparison with his late wife, you must try to learn how to make as good an apple pie as she did, and you must realize humbly that he probably married you only because you remind him of her.

Some widowers are genuinely worthy of pity, much more so, in fact, than any woman in the same situation. They are the ones who have no close relatives and no financial means and who, at the end of their lives, find themselves helplessly facing unmade beds, dusty rooms, dinners to be cooked and holes in their socks.

But there are also countless pathetic cases of old men who are of interest to no one since they are not completely penniless, and who are more likely to die of loneliness than of hunger. If you know men such as these, you ought to pay a visit this very day, bringing the comfort of a smile and perhaps an apple pie.

WIDOWS

Why, you may ask, should I talk about widows when they are by definition women who no longer have a man in their lives? Because there are more and more of them, they are very likely to need a man (or men), and it seems to me unfair for men to forget that they may one day leave their wives in this awkward position.

It is true that women are more adaptable than anyone else on earth. Since widowhood has become so common, they are no longer recluses as they used to be, melancholically trailing long black veils; even in India the bereaved wife no longer throws herself on her husband's funeral pyre. On the contrary, enriched by experience and by their late husband's insurance policies, widows have become one of the most powerful economic forces in the nation, and a woman who has accumulated several widowhoods never fails to find a new husband whose greed is greater than his sense of superstition.

Of course a certain percentage of them are really inconsolable, and in losing their husbands they lose all interest in life. These are the sentimental, devoted, timid women who do not dare go out alone at night, drive a car or make any decision more important than what to have for dinner. They have spent their entire lives at home, looking after the welfare of their families, and they don't know how to do anything else. I know a few of these women and my heart bleeds for them, although it is always the most disconsolate among them who remarry the soonest, for it is the state of marriage that they miss even more than the presence of a particular individual. But I also know even more widows who, having been faithful, loving wives until the end, pull themselves together after the initial shock has worn off and finally experience the headiness of independent decisions and start to live new lives.

But when a couple is destroyed, how heart-rending, how painful and how lonely it is for the one who is left behind! The children are often married and sometimes live far away; friends very quickly tire of the role of sympathizers; regret and sadness are attractive to nobody, and pity soon changes to lassitude.

If this misfortune should befall one of your women friends, the best service you can render is to help her find some new interest in life – a dog, a trip, or bridge – and instead of weeping with her over a cup of tea, force her to go out, take her to the films, to the theatre, to a concert, persuade her to join a club where she will make new friends who will not talk about her sad loss. Do what you can to see that her evenings are not always spent alone, but don't invite her to your home too often, for the sight of a happy couple will only make her sadder. But after a little while do not exclude her from your dinner parties on the pretext that you cannot find an extra man to balance the seating arrangement; the presence of an extra woman has never spoiled a good dinner party.

After all this sadness, let's brighten up a bit by thinking of the widows of famous men who seek vengeance for the shadow in which they lived throughout a spouse's lifetime and who at last experience the glory of appearing on television to explain how they were an inspiration to their poet or painter husband, or even how they helped to win a general election. All of which finally leads one to believe that a woman almost always needs a man to help her to affirm her personality, during his lifetime or afterwards, and that it is, after all, better to be a widow than to be a virgin and martyr.

WOUNDS

Although women have often made a speciality of dressing the most horrible wounds that men inflict upon each other in the course of their various games, they are also past mistresses in the art of causing moral injuries.

Men are choir boys compared with women when it comes to letting fly a brilliantly cruel remark – one that is certain to pierce the victim's heart, like a well-aimed poison arrow.

WRINKLES

I cannot remember who said that beyond a certain age we have the faces we deserve. A man whose face is marked with the attractive lines of one who has laughed a lot and loved a lot is absolutely irresistible (one more injustice), but a woman has to enjoy leading men on a leash in order to fall in love with one whose skin hangs in pitiful folds like the cocker spaniel that is disappointed because you have prevented him from sleeping in your best armchair; or she has to enjoy getting hurt in order to accord more than a single rendezvous to a man whose practically smooth face and steely eye eloquently proclaim that he never feels the slightest emotion. The miser, who cannot bear to give anything away – not even human kindness or a smile – has a mouth as shrunken as a chicken's crop with wrinkles all around; the drunk has pockets under his eyes; the playboy, dark circles; the idiot, a smooth brow, drooping mouth and round eye.

It is permissible to make a mistake in the choice of a very young man whose face has not yet been marked by the life he leads, but ageing Dorian Grays cannot keep their vices secret.

So open your eyes. Beyond a certain age, men cannot conceal everything from us.

X-RAYS

A few gifted people are able to read other people's minds; but if this technique were as widespread as X-rays, civilization would undoubtedly have to be entirely reconstructed on a new basis.

YAWNS

Yawning means that a person is bored, sleepy or hungry; when you are very excited by an idea or by a man, you never feel like yawning.

Basically, we live through life as we live through an evening: either we can yawn or we can shake ourselves out of it. In any case it is better to yawn from fatigue than from boredom.

(See also Boredom)

YES

This little word can lead to great consequences, and you should pronounce it only after due reflection.

'Yes, I love you. Yes, I'll marry you. Yes, I'll buy this object that I can't afford. Yes, I'll have another piece of chocolate cake. Yes, I'm leaving. Yes, I'm staying. Yes . . . yes . . . yes.'

Sometimes it would be wiser to say, 'No . . . no . . . no.'

YOUTH

What is there to say about youth that has not already been said and repeated a hundred times? That it is marvellous, that it is the only period when love is photogenic, that it is at the same time cruel and touching, that it is nothing to brag about because the most impoverished mortals have it too, that it passes quickly, that everyone regrets it? Yes, youth is all that. As soon as we have lost it, we try to console ourselves by saying that youth is mainly a state of mind. This is a little bit true – just as lump roe is a little bit like genuine caviare!

ZEST

This word, which is applied to so many advertised products and their enlightened users, suggests a person who is keen and lively. Having zest is the equivalent of having chic. It is expressing oneself in an amusing manner, avoiding trite phrases and ideas, deciding on a trip on the spur of the moment, enthusiastically accepting a new job, taking Russian lessons at the age of fifty, surrounding oneself with young people. It is, in short, having an appetite for life.

ZIPPER

It seems that one of the most common themes of masculine nightmares is having the zipper on their trousers get stuck! You can save your husband from a nervous breakdown very cheaply by slipping two little safety-pins into his wallet. And if the worst comes to the worst, a bit of soap applied to the offending metal can often work wonders. Sometimes men discover this all by their desperate selves, but if you plant the tip they'll be forever – if silently – grateful.

ZODIAC

Men believe in astrology rather less than we do be-ause they pride themselves on being strong-willed. But when they see us absorbed in reading our horo-scopes they seldom fail to ask with carefully assumed indifference: 'By the way, what does it say about Taurus?'

ZOOLOGY

It isn't difficult to imagine most men as members of the animal kingdom:

Here is the rooster, mounted on his spurs, who crows at the top of his lungs so that people will forget he is only a small bird; he fairly bursts with his own importance and is often as insufferable as he is intelligent.

Here is the peacock, a handsome man with a superb physique, who holds forth in front of the fireplace with his thumbs in the armholes of his waistcoat.

Here is the lion, serenely authoritative, naturally imposing, even pompous, and not always very clever.

Here is the monkey, who is always up to monkey-shines.

Here is the rat, with pointed chin and evasive eye, who scrounges and unearths all sorts of rottenness.

Here is the old goat with pointed beard, lewd remarks, wandering hands and a piggish eye.

Here is the fox, who sees all and who extricates himself from the most perilous situations with a pirouette.

Here is the cocker spaniel, humble, snivelling and jowly.

Here is the eagle, who awaits the first sign of weakness on your part in order to tear you to pieces.

Here is the St Bernard, a former lover on whom you can always count.

But you, mesdames, are you sure you don't resemble . . .

—a bleating lamb, curly-haired and destined to be gobbled up by a wolf?

— a mean and stupid goose, who struts about in society?

— a tiny black ant, active and avaricious?

— a cheerful grasshopper, unconcerned about the future?

— a placid cow, with huge udders and a dull eye, who ruminates all day long?

— a serpent who bites when one least expects it?

— or, in the best of roles, a mother hen who defends her brood, with feathers unfurled at the slightest sign of danger or even criticism?